Gratitude *with* Grace

MOSAICA PRESS

Gratitude *with* Grace

An Inspirational and Practical Approach
to Living Life as a Gift

SARAH S. BERKOVITS

Published by Mosaica Press, Inc.
www.mosaicapress.com
info@mosaicapress.com

In honor of

Sarah Berkovits

TEBAH EDUCATIONAL SERVICES

This book is dedicated with deep-felt love
to my esteemed parents

Rabbi Moshe Dovid *ben* Dov, *z"l*
Rebbetzin Chana *bas* Yosef, *z"l*
Berkovits

who made many sacrifices for Yiddishkeit
and taught me and my siblings, by word and action,
what it means to be a Jew.

In loving memory of our esteemed parents

Eliezer *ben* Ichel and Golda *bat* Baruch Berkovits
Moshe Chaim *ben* Baruch and Ella *bat* Israel Ehrlich

VERA BERKOVITS-EHRLICH AND BERNARD EHRLICH

Yitzchak A. Breitowitz

Michtav Berachah

The Sefas Emes raises an interesting question. Why are Jews called Yehudim? After all, Yehudah was only one of the twelve tribes. He explains that Leah named her fourth son Yehuda because *"Ha'paam* [now] *odeh es Hashem"*—now she can give full thanks to Hashem. The Midrash explains that Leah knew there would be twelve tribes emerging from four mothers so each mother was, as it were, entitled to three sons. When one gets what they think is coming to them, they do not necessarily feel gratitude; when Leah had son number four—more than her allotment—then and only then was her heart filled with gratitude. *"Natalti yeser al chelki."* The Sefas Emes says every Jew is a *Yehudi* because all of us at all times and under all conditions must have that very same feeling: God has given me more good than I deserve. Thus, the very term Jew, the essential characteristic of being a Jew—the simple meaning of the word is to be a grateful person, grateful to the Almighty for the gifts of life and all its blessings, grateful to our fellow human being for all they do.

Sadly, however, we live in a culture of entitlement. We expect things to go exactly the way we want them to go, and when there are setbacks, we get angry, frustrated, and resentful. We can be so fixated, even obsessed, with what we don't have that we do not appreciate all that we do have. This is not only a defect in character; it is a recipe for an unsatisfied, unfulfilled life. As the Alter of Slobodka put it, these bad *middos* not only destroy our *Olam Haba*, they make our *Olam Hazeh* pretty depressing as well. Conversely, a person who has internalized the *middah* of *hakaras hatov* is a happier person, a more resilient person, a person better equipped to deal with the vicissitudes of life, a person who will not be destroyed when things don't go exactly as planned. Once again, the values that the Torah promotes lead to well-adjusted psychological health. The grateful person is not only good and virtuous but strong, vibrant, and happy.

Ms. Sarah Berkovits, a psychologist with many years of experience working with youth, has authored a lovely book, developing these themes in great detail. Drawing on many Jewish sources, and supplemented by works of psychology, ethics, and creative literature, she demonstrates the importance of gratitude, the practical benefits gratitude can bring to your life and the techniques to develop a "grateful personality," including the raising of grateful children. What is especially useful is the inclusion at the end of each chapter of imagery exercises, concrete steps to turn theory into practice. As *Sefer HaChinuch* teaches, *"Adam nifal kefi peulosav"*—we **can** change our inner emotional orientation by repetitive virtuous action, and Ms. Berkovits shows us how to do it.

This is a topic of such surpassing importance and the author does such a superlative job of addressing it that all I can do is express my own gratitude for the great gift she has given me and every reader fortunate enough to pick up this book. It will make you a better person, it will make you a happier person, and you will be closer to Hashem. What could be better than that?

With much *berachah*,

Yitzchak A. Breitowitz
Rav, Kehillas Ohr Somayach, Jerusalem, Israel

David Pelcovitz, PhD

Psychologist
29 North Drive Great Neck, NY 11021

Reading *Gratitude with Grace* by Sarah Berkovits made me happy. The combination of anecdotes and practical recommendations on how to achieve a deep sense of gratitude in one's daily life is inspiring. I found myself immediately captivated by this book's engaging style, clarity, and comprehensive approach to gratitude—perhaps the most central value in Judaism. The many benefits of gratitude in promoting happiness, including improved sleep and immune functioning, are also carefully summarized.

One of the unique characteristics of this book is the unusually wide range of sources. Ms. Berkovits relies on wisdom ranging from secular authors such as Camus and Schweitzer, *mussar* teachers like Rav Wolbe and Talmudic scholars like Rav Shach. The wide array of topics covered in this book include the role of gratitude in dealing with adversity, parenting, teaching, and prayer. Every chapter ends with practical recommendations on how to integrate the lessons of that chapter into daily life through a combination of imagery, cognitive awareness, and practical interventions based on research in the area of positive psychology and writings based on Jewish sources.

Ms. Berkovits shares how powerful gratitude is in her own life in dealing with a wide range of challenges she faced in dealing with her own medical adversities and loss. Her honesty and self-awareness serve as a powerful model for integrating the many lessons of this book in dealing with life's inevitable stress and difficulty.

I strongly recommend this book to anybody looking for a guide to a deeper understanding of a value that has been found to be an antidote for many of the challenges posed by today's stressful world.

David Pelcovitz, PhD
Straus Chair in Psychology and Education,
Azrieli Graduate School, Yeshiva University, New York, NY

Imagine you are a 24-carat golden menorah
radiating your pure divine light into your heart
see and sense the light filtering down into your limbs
having a positive effect on your emotions and actions
Imagine you have inside yourself
a little garden, a patch of grass,
a blossoming orange tree with flowers and fruits
and four walls of green leaves around the garden
you are sitting by the tree
smell the fragrance of the flowers and imagine you are tasting the fruit
see the pure blue light from the sky passing through the leaves of the tree
pouring golden coins of light on the grass
sense the energy coming from the earth and the sky
entering you and passing through you
sense the blue light from the sky passing
through the leaves and entering you
sense the oxygen that is coming from the leaves energizing you
now visualize a disagreement or argument with a loved one
hear the voices rising
but you are in your personal Garden of Eden for now
with this strength you are able to answer your loved one
in a different manner than before
see and hear how you are doing this
what are you saying?
Notice the tone of your voice
What is happening?
Know that your personal Garden of Eden is always there for you
to calm, relax, refresh, and center you.
Be abundantly GRATEFUL

Table of Contents

My name is Devora. I am 11 years.
Having gratitude is important
because some peaple are very
grumpy and complain. peaple
would not want to be friends
whith them. But a drop of gratitud
could change their wrold around, and
make them a happy person. Also,
Having gratitude tells peaple they you
like and apreceate them.

Foreword

THE PRACTICE OF GRATITUDE

I am proud to be asked to provide a foreword for Sarah's inspiring book. As both a psychiatrist and a teacher, I found in this book a treasure trove of personal anecdotes, of homilies, and above all, of letters and pictures provided by Sarah's own pupils. These disadvantaged four-to-fourteen-year-olds were asked the central question: What am I grateful for? Some of their answers were so profound and so poignant that they made me weep.

With her own generosity, wisdom, and humor, Sarah has enchanted her pupils, who call her "Miss Fun." Eleven-year-old Yakov is thankful for waking up in the morning "because if I don't live how will I know anybody?" (Orthodox Jews, of course, start the day with thanks to the Almighty, who has given to the cock the intelligence to distinguish between day and night.) A fitting tribute to Sarah came from Ness: "Dear Ms. Berkovits, you were and still are the best person I ever met, so I will never forget you, even if I am married..."

Jewish liturgy is, of course, permeated with gratitude, but Sarah also draws on secular and humanist sources including Kant, Camus, Hume, Schweitzer, Proust, and Seneca. Her writing is not merely contemplative. On the contrary, she provides detailed action plans for cultivating and enhancing the practice of gratitude in our daily lives. These strategies include guided imagery and gratitude poems, pictures, journals, and letters (handwritten, of course, rather than impersonal and mechanical emails).

Finally, as a psychiatrist, I must endorse Sarah's erudite references to the scientific literature on gratitude. Recent research in the neurosciences demonstrates that gratitude increases the levels of "feel good" neurotransmitters including serotonin, dopamine, and endorphins.

I am certain that all Sarah's readers will be profoundly grateful for this book, which will be an endless source of appreciation of the vital spark in all other people and of acknowledgment of the infinite pleasure of creation.

Maurice Lipsedge
Consultant and Clinical Senior Lecturer,
Guy's King and St. Thomas' School
of Medical Education, London

Preface

*The greatest thing is to give thanks
for everything. He who has learned this
knows what it means to live. He has
penetrated the whole mystery of life:
giving thanks for everything.*

Albert Schweitzer

SIX YEARS AGO, on my way to the school where I worked as a guidance counselor, I fell on the ice and broke my hip and my wrist. I underwent two surgeries, followed by intensive physical therapy to learn how to walk again and to strengthen my arm. I spent eight days in the Hospital for Joint Diseases in Manhattan, followed by a stint of three weeks in a nursing rehabilitation facility in Brooklyn.

People from my community rallied around me. I had a constant stream of visitors in the nursing home and afterward when I returned home. They brought chocolates, flowers, newspapers, books, and CDs; a friend of a friend (whom I didn't even know) brought soup. My cousin sent cut-up watermelon, just what I needed to soothe my parched throat. My sister visited me on a daily basis, bringing delicious homemade dishes, and she spent Shabbos with me. She took me down in my wheelchair in the Shabbos elevator so I could daven (pray) in the facility's synagogue and enjoy the Shabbos meal with Kiddush and *zemiros* (table songs) with a few other patients, rather than be secluded in my room on the eighth floor.

My heart is full of gratitude to my sister and to all the people who visited me to lift my spirits. When I left the nursing home, Satmar Bikur Cholim[1] delivered tasty meals twice a week. On the rare occasions when they didn't, the kind rebbetzin of my shul sent one of her grandchildren to bring me home-cooked food, including fried fish, which I love. A friend offered to do my laundry until I was able to get back on my feet. Another friend called me daily, and sometimes even twice a day, for months, to make sure I was OK and had everything I needed.

I do not have enough words to express the gratitude in my heart and adequately thank each and every one of the members of my wonderful community who were there for me during this very trying time in my life. May God help you the way you helped me. May He provide for you the way you provided for me. May He lift your spirits the way you lifted mine.

I am extremely thankful to Hashem that He sent me to a very competent surgeon who operated on me with great skill and always treated me with patience, respect, and compassion. I owe him a great debt of gratitude.

Ten months after my fall, as I was returning home from the Friday night meal at my friends' home, I was struck by an SUV. I lay in the street in agony, crying out, "Call Hatzalah! Call Hatzalah!"[2] The minutes until the volunteer EMTs arrived seemed interminable, and I was petrified that another car would unwittingly drive over me and kill me. Later, I was informed that such an event had happened to a gentleman who was struck down on a nearby street; he was killed not by the first car that hit him, but by the second. While deeply sorry for his misfortune, I felt so much gratitude that this had not happened to me. I kept asking myself, *Why did God give me extra years? What am I supposed to do with them?*

And then one day the answer came: *You need to write a book on gratitude, to share your experiences, your thoughts, and your research findings with your community, as a way of expressing your hakaras hatov to Hashem (gratitude to God) and to all the people who were there for you.*

---

1   A volunteer aid society.
2   A volunteer medical emergency service.

You will see a number of children's drawings and writings throughout the book. Please do not be misled, the book is not intended for children, nor is it about children; it is intended for adults. I have included the drawings because they add charm, humor, and in some places, poignancy. And because I have learned so much about resilience and gratitude from the way these children express their feelings. Take, for example, nine-year-old Alex whose mother died when he was seven. He wrote, "I am thankful for my mother, for that she taught me good stuff. She died two years ago. She had cancer of the leg, she couldn't walk. I remember she had long hair but it fell off."

Use this book to assist you in developing your own practice of gratitude. Consider it your companion on a journey that will deepen your capacity for love, joy, and happiness, and strengthen your connection to God.

Writing this book is an act of gratitude on my part, in appreciation for the countless blessings I've experienced and continue to experience on a daily basis.

I WROTE THIS BOOK prior to the COVID-19 pandemic. It is my sincere hope that, in spite of all the pain and suffering it caused, you will nonetheless be able to take away many life-altering lessons of gratitude from these chapters.

I was at my local supermarket one morning in October 2020. Waiting in line to pay, I noticed a young man wearing a yarmulke, who was standing six feet behind me in order to comply with the coronavirus regulations. I was thinking about how the pandemic might alter our lives. Turning to him, I asked, "What do you think we should take away from this stressful time when it is all over?" He thought for a moment and then said, "Connection. To connect more to people." Pointing to his masked face, he added, "And to be careful how we speak."

"Yes," I replied. "Hopefully, when life gets back to normal, we will also have become more grateful human beings."

- Grateful for the countless everyday things we have taken for granted, never giving them much thought because we always had them, like being able to go to shul and pray, or being able to have family and friends join us for a Shabbos or Yom Tov meal

- Grateful for being able to ride buses and the subway without fear of becoming infected with this life-threatening virus, to go to the library, visit a museum, meet a friend for lunch or brunch in a restaurant
- Grateful to be able to go to work, if we are fortunate enough to still have a job, that our children can go to school, that we can hug a cherished friend or family member
- Grateful that we can attend a lecture or Torah class to expand our minds and nourish our souls
- Grateful that we can celebrate a bar or bas mitzvah or wedding and invite all our family members and friends without having to exclude any of them, and that we can travel abroad to participate in family *simchahs* (celebrations)

It goes without saying that we must feel endless gratitude that we survived, when hundreds of thousands didn't. It would indeed be a colossal mistake if, after the dust settles, we slide back into taking our life for granted, forgetting to feel thankful in our hearts, and forgetting to take that extra minute or two to find the best possible way to express our gratitude. The pandemic will be over. Let us make sure that our feelings of deep gratitude remain with us, every day without fail, for the rest of our lives.

Adversity brings with it opportunity. The opportunity of the moment is to realize, more profoundly than ever before, how blessed and privileged we are, how beloved by Almighty God, our Father, our Creator and Creator of the Universe, and then find ways to give back. As the Talmud says: "He is merciful, so too be merciful; He is gracious, so too be gracious."[3] We might add: He forgives, so too forgive; He is patient, so too be patient.

This is our challenge, to act with kindness and compassion to all God's creatures. Let us use this moment to translate our gratitude into action and make an everlasting commitment to do so every day of our lives.

Sarah S. Berkovits

---

3   *Shabbos* 133b.

Acknowledgments

I CAN'T ADEQUATELY EXPRESS my deep thanks to the people who graciously took an interest in me and my work but I will try—for I am truly grateful.

To Cathleen O'Connor, for generously reading the entire manuscript and giving helpful suggestions, and for your kind, supportive, encouraging words, at all times.

To Yitta Halberstam-Mandelbaum, my compassionate, devoted, decades-long friend, for reading the manuscript, offering helpful feedback, and for believing in me as a writer.

To Rabbi Yitzchak Breitowitz, Rebbetzin Tziporah Heller-Gottlieb, Dr. David Pelcovitz, Professor Tal Ben-Shahar, and Dr. Maurice Lipsedge, for taking the time to read the entire manuscript and for endorsing this book.

To Leah Mark, for decades of loyal friendship, for reading and editing the entire manuscript and making helpful suggestions, for your amazing generosity, and for taking an interest in my professional growth.

To my brothers Benzion and Shia, extraordinary Torah scholars, for supplying many of the sources.

To Nina Indig, for your very skillful and meticulous editing. It has been a pleasure working with you from beginning to end.

My deepest gratitude to Tat Chiu, for accompanying me on my journey, making yourself available at all times, keeping me on track, and helping me with the computer. Without your assistance, this book would have taken much longer to see the light of day.

To sponsors Rabbi Moshe Shamah, Morris Dweck, and Tebah Educational Services, for your recognition of the importance of my project, and magnanimous support toward the publication of this book from inception to completion, my deepest gratitude.

To Kess Family Fund, Dr. Bernard and Vera Ehrlich, Dr. Alan Waldman, and Frank Storch, my appreciation for your generous contributions. If I have inadvertently omitted anyone, I humbly ask for forgiveness and grace.

To Rabbi Doron Kornbluth, co-founder of Mosaica Press; Sherie Gross, managing editor; Rayzel Broyde, gifted art director; and the rest of the capable staff.

I am immensely grateful to God for giving me the idea, the time, and the wherewithal to write this book, and I am deeply grateful that I was the beneficiary of countless acts of Divine Providence (*hashgachah pratis*) along the way. Above all, I am grateful that the process of working on this project has made me a more consciously grateful person.

CHAPTER 1

The What and Why of Gratitude

Gratitude unlocks the fullness of life. It turns what we have into enough, and more. It turns denial into acceptance, chaos into order, confusion into clarity. It turns problems into gifts, failures into success, the unexpected into perfect timing, and mistakes into important events. Gratitude makes sense of our past, brings peace for today and a vision for tomorrow.

Melody Beattie

Gratitude: The quality or feeling of being grateful or thankful.

The Random House Dictionary of the English Language

An empathic emotion felt after receiving help from another, a moral virtue, an attitude toward a gift, an expression of thankfulness that promotes reciprocity, a sense of appreciation, a source of human strength.

Richard S. Lazarus and Bernice N. Lazarus[1]

---

1 *Passion and Reason: Making Sense of Our Emotions* (New York: Oxford University Press, 1994).

1

Synonyms: appreciation, thankfulness, gratefulness, recognition, indebtedness, acknowledgment, admiration.

Antonyms: thanklessness, ungratefulness, unappreciativeness, boorishness, callousness, unthankfulness.

Etymology: Old Latin: *gratus* (thankful, pleasing), which has its roots in *gratia* (favor, pleasing quality, or goodwill). In Sanskrit, the word *grnati* means "sing praise." In Lithuanian, *gririu* means to "praise" or "celebrate." During the thirteenth century, the short prayer before meals came to be called Grace. Gratitude makes one want to express appreciation or sing praise (*grnati*), even though no appreciation is expected. It is that sense of thanks one has for blessings or gifts received for which nothing is expected in return.

The origin of the word "thank" is interesting. It is derived from *pancian*, an Anglo-Saxon word which means to "give thanks." *Panc* is the root of the word "think." So giving thanks and thinking are connected. Gratitude comes from thinking about what and who have enriched your life.

GRATITUDE IS...

Gratitude is an emotion that involves a pleasant feeling that can occur when you receive a favor or benefit from another person. It is often accompanied by a desire to thank them or to reciprocate for a favor they have done for you. In a religious context, gratitude can also refer to a feeling of indebtedness toward a deity; for example, the expression of gratitude to God is a central theme in many, if not most, religions.

Gratitude is a sense of thankfulness that we have for someone or something or life in general. We can express it in thought, in word, or in deed. We cultivate it by training our eyes to focus on the good in people and in life situations.

Gratitude is a feeling, an attitude, and a state of being. It is an affirmation of the goodness in one's life and the recognition that the sources of this goodness lie at least partly outside the self. It is a very social experience, and it is restorative in times of stress.[2]

---

2   R. A. Emmons and C. M. Shelton, "Gratitude and the science of positive psychology," in

Gratitude is associated with happiness, positive mood, optimism, self-actualization, smooth interpersonal relationships, and a sense of community.[3]

DELVING DEEPER

How does one cultivate an attitude of gratitude? I wondered. Why is it important? What place does gratitude have in the Jewish religion? What do our great rabbis and Jewish philosophers teach us about gratitude? What does scientific research have to say about gratitude? Further, I asked myself, is gratitude possible in the face of adversity?

BE AWARE

Rabbi Shlomo Wolbe[4] notes that the prerequisite of joy is awareness. Joy is not the result of having more things but of having more awareness of what we already have. Such awareness will lead us to feel gratitude, which is an important dimension of life as we interact with one another in our everyday affairs.

We can stimulate the feeling of gratitude when we decide to look for the good in people, in things, and in situations. This is what it means to have an *ayin tovah* (a good eye). With the correct intention and with practice, our grateful feelings turn into a state of mind, and this is how we cultivate an attitude of gratitude.

The more I thought about gratitude and the more I practiced it, the happier I became. I was calmer, I slept better, and my interpersonal relationships gradually improved. I began to find the good in almost every situation. That is not to say every situation was good, but somehow, without me even trying, something good would pop into my head about untoward circumstances. For example, when my air conditioner broke and I was extremely uncomfortable on a very hot and humid day, I found myself saying, "Thank God it didn't break yesterday when I had company."

C. R. Snyder and S. J. Lopez (Eds.), *Handbook of Positive Psychology* (Oxford: Oxford University Press, 2002), pp. 459–471.

3   Ibid.

4   Renowned *Mashgiach* (spiritual guide of yeshiva students) and author of *Alei Shur*, a *mussar* classic discussing dimensional growth as it pertains to students of the Talmud (1914–2005).

Or when my elevator broke down for the umpteenth time, I found myself saying, "Thank God it didn't happen yesterday when I came home loaded with bags of shopping."

POSITIVE SPEECH

As I focused more on gratitude, I began to say positive things to people I encountered as I went about my day. The smiles I brought to their faces made me at least as happy as I made them.

I started to adequately thank the janitors in the schools in which I worked. "Thank you for keeping the building so spotlessly clean—the floors glisten. By your hard work you create a pleasant environment for us, so teachers are able to teach better, and students to learn more." Grinning from ear to ear, they always thank me for thanking them. It adds such richness to my day.

I thank the bus driver before getting off the bus. It's not an easy job they have. Buses get crowded and are often very noisy, especially when schoolchildren ride to or from school. There's traffic to contend with, as well as double-parking in certain neighborhoods. It is true that they get paid for their work, but we benefit and need to say thank you. I don't merely say thanks; I usually add, "You're a great driver." It's amazing how adding those few words makes them feel appreciated. They usually wish me a good day and thank me for thanking them. It's not uncommon for gratitude to beget gratitude in return.

I thank the security guard as I enter the school building. "Thank you for keeping us safe. Every teacher and every student appreciates that you show up each morning to help us."

I thank the mail carrier. "On behalf of our community, thank you for bringing our mail to us no matter what the weather. You people are amazing!" They deliver our mail every day; they need to be thanked every day.

TAKING STOCK

As the day unfolds, periodically pause for a moment or two—or three or four—to take stock of the blessings in your life. Ask yourself, "To whom am I grateful? For what am I grateful? Have I expressed today my thanks and appreciation to my spouse, my child, my coworkers, my boss? To God?"

You may want to make a list, as I do, of the things you're grateful for on each particular day, all the things that went well. Read your list before going to bed. Don't be surprised if you find yourself sleeping better!

As you come up with your own distinct way to work with gratitude, become aware of how the practice will literally change your life. This book contains suggested gratitude practices and imagery exercises to help you develop an attitude of gratitude. Try out the exercises and see what happens. See if you feel more peaceful, if your day seems calmer, if you are more easily able to get along with others.[5]

Warm-Ups

To sharpen your senses and improve your ability to image, here are some warm-up exercises. Do as many of them as you wish. You may want to take several days to do them all.

Imagine you are **hearing**...

...a door slam / the sound of a waterfall / a dog barking / a cat meowing / crickets chirping at night / a mosquito buzzing / the humming of an air conditioner / a gardener mowing the lawn / the screech of a car coming to a sudden halt / the shrill sound of an ambulance / a favorite piece of music / yourself singing a song you like / the phone ringing / the doorbell buzzing / the pages of a newspaper rustling / your car idling / the chiming of a grandfather clock / the sound of thunder / your child's voice / birds trilling / the wind howling / the patter of raindrops on your roof / a ball bouncing / the rustling of autumn leaves...

Imagine you are **touching**...

...velvet / sandpaper / a wooden door / a metal door / a window pane / the door of your refrigerator / a silk garment / a polyester shirt / a woolen jacket / hot water / cold water / tepid water / a block of ice / a sheet of paper / a hairbrush / a comb / fur / the bark of a tree / a leaf / your hair / the soft skin of a newborn infant...

Imagine you are **tasting**...

---

5   For a fuller discussion of imagery, see chapter 2.

...your favorite flavor of ice-cream / a slice of pizza / a bar of chocolate / corn on the cob / mashed potatoes / roasted potatoes / sushi / falafel / a leafy salad / a slice of toast / pea soup / chicken soup / roast chicken straight from the oven / a doughnut / a cup of coffee / a slice of lemon / scrambled eggs / olives / pickled cucumbers / jalapeño peppers / horseradish...

Imagine you are **seeing**...

...yourself in the mirror / a bird building a nest / the traffic light changing color / a magnolia tree in full bloom / an arcade of cherry blossom trees in the botanical gardens / dogwood trees resplendent in color in somebody's garden / a mother walking her young child to school / a squirrel scampering up a tree / a favorite painting / fall foliage / a field of daffodils / a family photo / shelves of books in the library...

Imagine you are **smelling**...

...the aroma of freshly brewed coffee / the magnificent scent of a rose / fish frying in the kitchen / your favorite perfume / a perfume you don't like / fresh country air / talcum powder / a tire burning / the smell of gasoline when filling your car / cake baking in the oven / jasmine / honeysuckle / sulfur / spices you like / rosemary / a lemon / milk turned sour / gas leaking from your stove / freshly laundered linen / burnt toast / garlic / peppermint / mold / lavender / ocean air / turpentine / ammonia / cloves / freshly mowed grass...

RANDOM ENCOUNTERS

Being naturally interested in people and curious about what things they might be grateful for, I began, over a period of a few months, to initiate brief conversations with people I encountered on the train, bus, or subway platform, and even people I met in the street. I'd greet them with a smile and ask if they had a minute or two to spare. After explaining that I was an author writing a book on gratitude, I'd invite them to share some things for which they were thankful.

During those brief encounters, I gained a measure of insight into what people appreciate. The experiment was most enriching. It broadened my horizons and gave me ideas about how to become more appreciative for the things I have and also for what I don't have; for carrots and water, as my friend Denise told me; for each time someone held the door open for me, as my student with spina bifida said. I learned so much from the person who was schizophrenic, depressed, and bipolar, yet found something to be thankful for in spite of it all.

I bring some of their responses in this book, as well as children's drawings and letters I collected during my years as a teacher and therapist, to provide you with more ideas of things to appreciate in your lives. See what else you can come up with. Keep a book handy in which to write your ideas. Make it a daily practice. And don't be surprised if you notice yourself becoming calmer, more compassionate, happier, and more joyful in the process.

Gratitude Practices

- Every day, identify someone for whose existence you feel grateful. Tell them this and tell them why.
- Make a collage of things for which you are grateful. Cut out pictures from a magazine, or draw them. Place your collage in a prominent place where you will see it—for example, on your bathroom mirror, bedroom door, or refrigerator. You could make several different collages—one for things you're grateful for, one for people you're grateful for, and one for experiences and situations for which you are grateful. You could also make a small version of your collages to carry around with you in your pocket or wallet so that each time you put your hand in your pocket, you'll be reminded of what you're grateful for.

I am thankful for my mom
that she gave birth to me
so now I am alive, and
for Hashem Being my God,
He gave me life, also, and
I'm thankful He made me
a Jew

David, 10

CHAPTER 2

Gratitude in Judaism

What can I give the Lord for all His
kindnesses He has given me?[1]

Tehillim (Psalms) 116:12

GIFT OF A NEW DAY

In 2005, a week before Pesach, my beloved brother Dayan Berel Berkovits went to sleep one night but didn't wake up in the morning, leaving a wife and four sons, the youngest not yet nine years old. I realized then in a more profound way than ever before what an amazing gift each day is, given to us gratuitously by the Creator of the world.

Jewish tradition teaches that every night our souls ascend to Heaven when we go to sleep, and God, in His goodness, restores them to us each morning when we awake. Perhaps we messed up yesterday, perhaps we were found lacking, perhaps we hurt somebody's feelings inadvertently, perhaps we acted with impatience or anger, perhaps we harbored resentment, held onto a grudge, were greedy or envious. Notwithstanding, God has granted us the gift of a new day. Each day is an opportunity for personal growth and accomplishment, for learning new things, for connecting to people, for sharing, for finding inner peace, and finding the good in ourselves and in others. Each new day brings the opportunity to attain greater spiritual heights, to experience love and to give love, to enjoy God's bountiful blessings—to hear birds singing and perhaps

---

1   Rabbi Elya Lopian would start every lecture he gave with these words.

watch one building its nest; to see the blue sky and the clouds, to smell the exquisite fragrance of flowers, to use our senses to enjoy their beauty, to touch their silky petals and marvel at their colors.

How grateful we have to be for this amazing gift! How appreciative that Almighty God desires to have a relationship with us; that, far from being insignificant, we are important to Him!

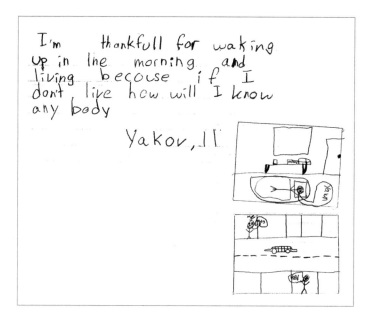

MODEH ANI

> *I give thanks before You, King Who lives and endures forever,*
> *because You have compassionately restored my soul to me,*
> *great is Your faithfulness.*

We recite the *Modeh Ani* prayer as soon as we open our eyes, even before getting out of bed, before washing our hands, brushing our teeth, or washing our face, before sipping our first cup of tea or coffee of the day. First and foremost, a Jew gives thanks to the Creator. Nothing is as important as giving thanks![2]

---

2   Chazal (our Rabbis) tell us that were all the sacrifices to be abolished in the future, the

We thank God for our souls, which are a part of God Himself. Just as God endures forever, so, too, our souls endure forever—and for this, too, we thank Him.

Every moment of every day is a gift from God, for which we owe a huge debt of gratitude. Were we to do nothing else the whole day but sing songs of praise to God and give thanks to Him, it would not be enough for the manifold benefits with which He blesses us, moment by moment by moment, day after day after day.

By saying *Modeh Ani,* we begin our day by focusing on how blessed we are. At that moment, we cannot complain about the things we don't have. Just as one cannot hear a Mozart symphony and Tchaikovsky's work simultaneously, it is impossible to feel two such different emotions at the same time. When we're grateful, we cannot be in a low mood. There are things we don't have, but why waste energy focusing upon them when we can, instead, focus our attention on how very blessed we are? When we concentrate on what we don't have, we rob ourselves of what we do have. When we focus on the good, we attract more good.

It takes me a long time to recite this short morning prayer consisting of only twelve words. I think about everything I am thankful for: people, situations, things, opportunities, experiences. I sing a personal song of gratitude to myself, mentioning everything for which I am grateful. I begin by listing all the people who have benefited me: my parents, ancestors, siblings, teachers, and friends, both past and current. I name each of them. I even express thanks for the new friends I anticipate making at some time in the future.

Modeh Ani concludes with the words "great is Your faithfulness." God has faith in me. Surely, then, I need to have faith in myself, to let self-doubt fall by the wayside. When this happens, miracles are possible.

I've often wondered why, in this prayer, we say, "*Modeh ani*—Thank I" instead of, "*Ani modeh*—I thank." We don't say, "*Kotev ani*—Write I," we say, "*Ani kotev*—I write." We don't say, "*Holech ani*—Walk I," we say, "*Ani holech*—I walk." In Hebrew syntax, just as in English, the

---

Korban Todah (thanksgiving sacrifice) would remain (*Midrash Tehillim* 100:4). That's how important gratitude is!

subject precedes the verb. So why in this prayer does the verb precede the subject?

The following thought came to me: gratitude is the foundation of everything. It's gratitude that creates the *ani*; it's gratitude that creates the person. Without gratitude, I'm an incomplete human being. It is through feeling gratitude and finding ways to express it that I become a person, worthy of the name human being.

In each person's life, challenges are bound to arise. Starting our day with *Modeh Ani* reminds us that God is with us, that we are not alone, and with this knowledge it is easier to face difficulties as they arise.

It is helpful to count our blessings. If we are among those people who can get out of bed in the morning and can see, hear, smell, touch, and taste; if we can prepare and enjoy a hot drink in the morning and are not dependent on others to make it for us; if we have a home, furniture, objects of beauty, family, and friends—surely this is cause for celebration! How blessed we are. What joy!

I Thank You God for Most This Amazing

i thank You God for most this amazing
day: for the leaping greenly spirits of trees
and a blue true dream of sky; and for everything
which is natural which is infinite which is yes

(i who have died am alive again today,
and this is the sun's birthday; this is the birth
day of life and of love and wings: and of the gay
great happening illimitably earth)

how should tasting touching hearing seeing
breathing any—lifted from the no
of all nothing—human merely being
doubt unimaginable You?

(now the ears of my ears awake and
now the eyes of my eyes are opened)

e. e. cummings

THE BASIS FOR OBSERVANCE

The first of the Ten Commandments is actually not a commandment, it's a statement: "I am the Lord your God, who brought you out of the land of Egypt, from the house of bondage."[3]

Isn't it interesting—the Bible doesn't say, "I am the Lord your God, who created the world." The emphasis is on God taking us out of Egypt, where, for 210 years, we were subjected to the worst kind of slavery. Our baby boys were cast into the Nile River to drown. We were tortured relentlessly. Thirty-three hundred years ago, Egypt was like the USSR of the twentieth century. It was impossible to escape from there. God performed a multitude of miracles for us in Egypt. He liberated us after performing the ten plagues. He gave us our freedom. He gave us the Torah. If we think about this, we come to realize that we owe God a huge debt of gratitude. Hence it is gratitude that serves as the basis for our observance of all of God's commandments.

One of the most important of these is the mitzvah (commandment) to honor one's parents. The *Sefer Hachinuch* teaches that the basis of this mitzvah is gratitude. Even if our parents have disappointed us or weren't always able to be there for us. Even if they were overly critical, we still owe them gratitude for bringing us into this world, taking care of us, feeding us, clothing us, making sure we are healthy, educating us, and providing for our multiple needs. Once we realize how grateful we need to be to our parents, we will come to be thankful to God, the Ultimate Giver.

According to *Ramban* (Nachmanides),[4] the world was created in order for us to express gratitude to God. A similar thought is expressed in *Midrash Bereishis Rabbah* 1:4, which states that one reason the world was created was for the sake of *bikkurim* (first fruits), which were brought to the Beis Hamikdash (Holy Temple) and given to the priests in gratitude for God's blessings.

The eleventh-century author Bachya ibn Pakuda teaches that the basis of our *avodas Hashem* (service of God) is *hakaras hatov*, showing

---

3   *Shemos* (Exodus) 20:2.
4   Ibid., 13:16.

gratitude to the Creator. In his *Chovos Halevavos* (Duties of the Heart), he thus expresses this concept:

> *Because You endure all, create everything out of nothing, and give life to all, and because everything comes from You and is among Your deeds, it is proper to praise You, it is pleasant to sing to You, it is becoming to thank You and good to chant to You. And though we know that praise is of no avail and chanting is of no consequence to You, nonetheless, our consciences make it incumbent upon us to repay You in kind for Your benevolence and wonders by offering as much praise, song, and gratitude as possible.[5]*

Ibn Pakuda makes the point that we owe thanks to people for a favor received even if the beneficiary is motivated by self-interest or egotistical reasons, and he extrapolates this: how much more so are we obligated to have gratitude to God!

Consequently, we should work on ourselves to inculcate the trait of gratitude into our personalities—gratitude to man and gratitude to God. In truth, we cannot adequately thank the Creator, Who gave us life and continues on a daily basis to give us life. The Almighty created the world for our benefit and enjoyment and performs miracles on a daily basis. However, as our Sages point out in the *Nishmas* prayer:

> *If our mouths were to be full of song as vast as the sea, and our tongues joyful as the multitude of waves, and our lips full of praise like the expanse of the firmaments, and our eyes bright as the sun and the moon, and our hands outstretched like the span of eagles' wings, and our feet swift as deer, we would not be able to sufficiently thank God for even one of the thousand thousand, thousands of thousands of favors He bestowed upon our forefathers and upon us.*

---

5   "The Tenth Gate: The Gate of the Complete Love of God" (translated by Yaacov Feldman).

God's kindnesses to us are so vast that it is impossible to thank Him sufficiently, nor praise Him adequately, for even one of the thousand millions of blessings He bestows on us. If we consider as separate gifts every moment of life for every Jew for the almost two thousand years from our forefather Avraham to the compilation of this prayer, the number is unfathomable.

Akdamus, echoing rabbinic phraseology, declares:

> *Could we with ink the ocean fill,*
>
> *Were every blade of grass a quill,*
>
> *Were the world of parchment made,*
>
> *And every man a scribe by trade—*
>
> *To write the love of God above*
>
> *Would drain that ocean dry;*
>
> *Nor would the scroll contain the whole*
>
> *Though stretched from sky to sky!*[6]

Our rabbis teach us that the world is a reflection of God's kindness and that we should train our eyes to see the beauty all around us. As Jews, our task is to understand that everything, and every moment, is a gift from God. Such an attitude will enhance our feelings of gratitude to the Creator. We will pray with more *kavanah* (focus), we will feel God's presence in our lives and feel closer to Him more often, we will be more joyful, and ultimately live more meaningful lives.

Rabbi Eliyahu Dessler, one of the foremost teachers of the Mussar movement, explains in *Michtav Me'Eliyahu* that faith in God and *hakaras hatov* are intertwined. If we believe in God, we recognize that He is responsible for all the good in our lives. This recognition should make us feel grateful to Him. Conversely, having *hakaras hatov* can lead us to acquire faith in God.

---

6   From *The Authorized Daily Prayer Book* with commentary by Rabbi Dr. J. H. Hertz (London, England), p. 419 (July 1946).

EMULATING GOD

We are supposed to emulate the traits we see in God, as the Torah says: "And you shall walk in His ways."[7] He is compassionate, so be compassionate; He is gracious, so be gracious. In the same vein, He is a giver, so we should become givers.

God shows *hakaras hatov* even to a dog. It says in the Bible: "And you shall be a holy nation unto Me; therefore, if an animal is killed in the field, you cannot eat it; throw it to the dog."[8] Why does the Torah single out the dog? The famous commentator *Rashi* explains that the Torah is teaching us a lesson that God does not withhold reward from any of His creatures. God says we are to give the dogs a reward because they didn't bark when the Jews left Egypt.

Dogs don't have free choice. It didn't require any effort on their part not to growl. However, God says they must be rewarded for that. From this we can extrapolate that gratitude is required even for seemingly insignificant things and even when the person from whom we received a favor didn't intend to do us a favor. We follow God's example when we act in this manner.

Expressing gratitude refines our character. We are told that the Torah's commandments were not given to mankind for any purpose other than to refine people.[9]

If someone helped us in some way or did us a favor and we didn't express appreciation, that person's feelings may be hurt. He may feel that he is being taken for granted. By showing *hakaras hatov*, we make our benefactors feel appreciated.

Still, gratitude is more than just saying thank you. It's a state of mind, it's a feeling, it's a sense of awe and wonder, it's a way of life, it's a connection to people and, ultimately, a deeper connection to God.

---

7   *Devarim* (Deuteronomy) 28:9, *Shabbos* 133b, *Sotah* 14a, *Rambam, Hilchos Dei'os* 1:5–6.
8   *Shemos* (Exodus) 22:30.
9   *Bereishis Rabbah* 44:1.

MATRIARCH OF GRATITUDE

Highly spiritual people often believe that the good they receive is more than they deserve. This is in stark contrast to people who feel entitled, that they never have been given enough, and that they always deserve more.

Our Sages teach us that we learn gratitude from our Matriarch Leah.[10] As a prophetess, Leah knew that Yaakov (Jacob) would sire twelve sons who would ultimately become the twelve tribes of Israel. Therefore, she anticipated that each of Yaakov's four wives would give birth to three sons. When she gave birth to a fourth son, she named him Yehudah, derived from the Hebrew root "to thank." When parents give a name to a child, they are guided by Divine providence to choose that particular name for that particular soul. Leah felt she had been given more than she deserved. Every time she called her son by name, she felt grateful, and feelings of gratitude would accompany her throughout her day. If we, like Leah, would feel that we have been given more than we deserve, we would always be grateful—and humble, too.

It is interesting to note that Mashiach (the Messiah), the ultimate redeemer of the world, will be a descendant of the tribe of Yehudah—the one whose name means gratitude. From here we see that gratitude brings redemption. By inculcating the fundamental character trait of gratitude into our psyches and consciously striving to translate these feelings into actions, we hasten the coming of Mashiach.

THE BEHAVIOR OF *YEHUDIM*

The Hebrew word for Jew is *Yehudi* and it means, "the one who gives thanks." That is our essence, who we are, and who we should strive to be at all times—always cognizant of the good we receive from God and the good we receive from man. No good is too minuscule for us to refrain from giving thanks.

As *Yehudim* ("those who are grateful"), Jews are enjoined to bring *bikkurim*, the first fruits we harvest, to the Beis Hamikdash (the

---

10   *Berachos* 7b.

Holy Temple).[11] We give them to the Kohanim (priests) as a token of gratitude for the bounty with which God has blessed us. Our natural tendency would be to taste the first fruits ourselves because of our excitement when we notice that they have ripened. However, we see that before we derive benefit from the fruits of our labor, we must thank the Creator, Who made it all possible. Gratitude must come before personal enjoyment.

That is not to say we shouldn't enjoy things. God wants us to enjoy, but only after we have given thanks to Him—only after we recognize the One Who bestows blessings upon us. And so, before we eat a morsel of food, we say the appropriate blessing, thanking God that He gives us such a variety of food, that the food tastes so good and looks so appetizing. After we have partaken of our food, we again thank God before leaving the table.

Our rabbis teach that we should recite one hundred blessings each day to serve as constant reminders to thank God.[12] We pray thrice daily—morning, noon, and night—thanking God for life, for the gift of each day, for every breath, for eyesight, for all our senses, for clothing and shoes, for food, for having been freed from slavery in Egypt 3,300 years ago. We never cease to be thankful for any good done to us, no matter how long ago it happened. We are enveloped in a blanket of gratitude from the moment we open our eyes in the morning to the time we close our eyes when retiring for the night, before dropping off to sleep.

MOSHE, OUR ROLE MODEL

We learn the importance of gratitude from Moshe Rabbeinu (Moses our teacher). He did not bring about the first three of the ten plagues; his brother, Aharon HaKohen (Aaron the priest), did. *Rashi* explains:[13]

- Moshe couldn't turn the Nile River into blood because of the role the river had played in saving his life. As a three-month-old infant, Moshe was placed in the river in a little basket to

---

11   *Devarim* 26:1–11.
12   *Menachos* 43b.
13   *Shemos* 7:19.

hide him from the Egyptians, who would have killed him had they found him. Because the water of the river saved him, he refrained from striking it eighty years later when he was sent to save the Jewish People.

- Moshe couldn't strike the earth to bring about the plague of lice because when he killed the Egyptian taskmaster who was beating a Jew, the earth covered the body, thereby concealing the evidence, preventing Pharaoh from punishing him.[14]

Water and earth do not have feelings; they don't get insulted. But someone who was destined to be the leader of the Jewish People had to avoid any act that had even the slightest semblance of ingratitude. If we have to show gratitude to inanimate objects, all the more so do we have to show gratitude to people and to God.

Gratitude is so important that Moshe taught it to us more than once. If we study the Biblical text, we see that he taught it to us a second and third time.[15] We learn from this that *hakaras hatov* must be practiced repeatedly until it becomes second nature.

When God instructed Moshe to go to Egypt to liberate the Jewish People from slavery, Moshe said that first he had to take leave of his father-in-law, Yisro (Jethro), to acknowledge the benefits Yisro had bestowed on him during his sojourn in Midian. Moshe felt he had to show gratitude to Yisro even before doing God's bidding. We see from this how extremely important expressing gratitude is. We also see that the process of redemption is built on the basis of *hakaras hatov*.

"*MODIM ANACHNU LACH*"—THE BLESSING OF THANKSGIVING

We give thanks unto You for You are the Lord our God and the God of our fathers forever and ever. You are the Rock of our lives, the Shield of our salvation through every generation. We will give thanks to You and declare Your praise for our lives, which are committed to Your Hand, and for our souls, which

---

14   *Shemos* 8:12.
15   When bringing about the plagues of blood, frogs, and lice.

are in Your charge, and for Your miracles, which are daily with
us, and for Your wonders and Your benefits, which are wrought
at all times, evening, morning, and noon. You Who are all good,
whose mercies do not fail, You merciful Being Whose loving-
kindnesses never cease, we have ever hoped in You.[16]

When praying in the synagogue with a quorum, it is customary for the cantor to repeat the *Shemoneh Esreh*.[17] This practice arose at the time when many people didn't know how to pray or when prayer books were not readily available. We can fulfill our obligation to pray by listening intently as the cantor recites each of the blessings and by saying amen after each blessing. Of course, it is preferable to verbalize our prayers ourselves, provided we can do so.

However, when it comes to the blessing of *Modim*, the blessing of thanksgiving, we cannot fulfill our obligation merely by listening to the chazzan; we must verbalize the blessing of *Modim* ourselves. That's how central gratitude is to our lives. We cannot delegate it to another person.

PRAYING WITH GRATITUDE

A man wished to see how the famed Chafetz Chaim prayed *Shemoneh Esreh*. He observed that the great sage took much longer to finish than all the other worshippers.

"What deep Kabbalistic *kavanos* (intentions) do you have when praying?" he asked.

The Chafetz Chaim replied, "No special deep *kavanos*. I go through the *Shemoneh Esreh* paying attention to every word. When I come to the prayer of *Modim*, I have so much to be thankful for that it takes me a good while. That's the reason I finish later than everybody else."

WHAT KIND OF BEING DO WE WISH TO BE?

A person who fails to appreciate the gifts, favors, benefits, kindnesses, and blessings he has received from people or from God is referred to as a *kefui tovah*. The word *kefui* comes from the same root letters as the

---

16   Rabbi Dr. J. H. Hertz, *The Authorized Daily Prayer Book.*
17   The eighteen-blessing silent prayer said three times daily, also known as the *Amidah.*

Hebrew word that means to "cover up" or to "bend." An ingrate covers up the good or he bends it. He doesn't want to be cognizant of it, let alone admit it. He doesn't wish to be beholden to anyone and he doesn't want to give back. He only wants to receive.

Rabbi Eliyahu Dessler teaches that the world is comprised of two kinds of people: takers and givers. Ask yourself: *Do I want to go down in history as a receiver, or do I want to be remembered as a giver?*

- When we appreciate the good someone does for us, we give back to them.
- When we fail to appreciate the good we receive, we easily sink to the level of ingrates.

Some people act as if life is about getting and having, but in truth, it's about being and giving. We each need to ask ourselves:

- What kind of human being do I wish to be?
- Do I strive to refine my character in order to reach greater spiritual heights, or am I complacent living my life without any desire to grow?

If we wish to refine our characters, the best place to begin is by working at becoming more grateful.

The Talmud speaks about two kinds of guests:

- A good guest thinks, "Look how much the host labored for me. Look at this amazing Shabbos meal."
- A bad guest says, "He didn't do it for me, he did it for his wife and children."[18]

Two people can go to the same house and partake of the same meal, yet one genuinely is grateful and thanks the host and the other neither feels nor shows any real gratitude at all.

---

18   *Berachos* 58a.

INGRATITUDE OF BIBLICAL PROPORTIONS

There is nothing harder for the Almighty to live with (as it were) than an ungrateful person.[19]

Let's take a look at the creation of Adam and Chavah (Adam and Eve) on the sixth day of Creation, recorded in the first chapter of the book of *Bereishis* (Genesis). We all know the story. God put them into Gan Eden (the Garden of Eden), the original paradise. "From all the trees of the garden you may eat," God said, "but from the tree of knowledge of good and evil you may not eat." The serpent enticed Chavah to eat the forbidden fruit, and she ate. She gave it to Adam, and he ate. Then God asked Adam, "Where are you? Did you eat from the tree from which I commanded you not to eat?" God is omniscient (all-knowing); of course He knew where Adam was physically! He was trying to get him to look at how far he had fallen spiritually. To which Adam replied, "The woman *You* gave to be with me gave me from the tree and I ate." By putting the blame on Chavah, Adam showed that he didn't appreciate her and that he didn't appreciate the gift God had given him by providing him with a companion for life. God wanted him to admit his sin, and He may have forgiven him had he done so. But Adam failed to do so. This blatant lack of gratitude was something God couldn't tolerate, and He exiled them from Gan Eden.

There is a lesson in this for all of us. When we are ungrateful, we hurt ourselves, because we exile ourselves from our own personal Gan Eden, our own paradise. Ungrateful people are ultimately unhappy people. Their relationships are bound to suffer because they fail to give credit where credit is due.

Pharaoh was the quintessential ingrate. He professed not to know Yosef.[20] How was this possible? How could he not know about Yosef? After all, Yosef saved his country from starvation during the years of famine! Everybody in Egypt knew about Yosef, as did all the surrounding nations. However, Pharaoh didn't want to acknowledge the amazing

---

19   *Pirkei d'Rabi Eliezer*, Chapter 7.
20   "And a new king arose who did not know Yosef" (*Shemos* 1:8).

benefits he and his nation had received on account of Yosef. He was a *kefui tovah*—an ingrate—par excellence. Ultimately, this led him to deny God, as we see from what he said: *"Mi Hashem*—Who is God, that I should listen to His voice to send out the nation of Israel? I do not know God, and I shall not let Israel leave."[21] One who denies the good he receives from man may end up denying the good he receives from God.

INTENT TO CHANGE

A person might be meticulous in observing the 613 commandments, but if he is an ingrate, his character is grossly flawed, and he can hardly be considered a good Jew.

It is true that some people are born with the character trait of gratitude, but those of us who are not can change our attitude and behavior, provided we are made aware—and are humble enough to admit—that we need to fix something. Once we recognize the flaw, we need to have a clear perception of what it is we want to change, and then we need to have the intention to do so. Without intention, we will not succeed. Judaism focuses on the importance of *kavanah* (having the proper intention). We are told that mitzvos require *kavanah*.[22]

We also need patience, perseverance, and constancy. Making an effort one day—or even two or three days—will not suffice. We need to make a concerted effort on a daily basis. It doesn't have to take long. A few minutes being mindful of our attitude and behavior can go a long way.

Improvement in any endeavor happens in increments. If you don't see desired results right away, don't give up. To change a habit is a lifetime's work.

There is a well-known story about a man who said he wanted to change his country. When he realized it was impossible, he said he wanted to change his city. Later he said he wanted to change his family. As he matured more, he realized his task on earth was to change himself.

Progress may be slow. In order not to feel discouraged, it is beneficial for us to acknowledge our successes, however small they may be. Each

---

21 *Shemos* 5:2.
22 *Berachos* 13a, *Eruvin* 95b, *Pesachim* 114b.

time we see the slightest improvement toward attaining our goal, we should say, "Well done, ____!" and add our name, or write ourselves little complimentary notes expressing how proud we are of our progress—and then read these notes periodically.

A baby doesn't learn to walk without falling. But each time she falls, she picks herself up and continues to try. When she takes her first tentative steps, everyone applauds, and this helps her to keep trying. We need to applaud, to cheer ourselves on as we move forward.

"*BIRKAS HAMAZON*"—TRUST IN GOD

> *We thank you, O Lord our God, because You gave as a heritage to our fathers, a desirable, good and ample land, and because You took us out from the land of Egypt, and delivered us from the house of bondage as well as for Your covenant which You have sealed in our flesh, Your Torah which You have taught us, your statutes which you have made known to us and for life, grace and loving kindness which You have bestowed upon us, and for the food by which You constantly feed and sustain us on every day, in every season, at every hour. For all this, O Lord our God we thank and bless You, blessed be Your name by the mouth of all living continually and forever...Blessed are You, O Lord for the land and for the food.*[23]

Expressing gratitude is linked to *bitachon* (trust in God). We see this concept expressed in *Birkas Hamazon* (Grace after Meals). We thank God for all the good He has done for us in the past and does for us in the present, and express faith that He will, in the future, continue to bestow goodness upon us.

On a moment-by-moment basis, God acts toward us with compassion and kindness. As I *bentched* (recited *Birkas Hamazon*) one morning after breakfast, the words, "the King Who is good and Who does good to all beings, He has done good, He does good, and He will do good to us," jumped out at me, making me realize how much we have to be grateful

---

23   Rabbi Dr. J. H. Hertz, *The Authorized Daily Prayer Book.*

for. God showers us with love and gives us opportunities to return to Him, should we stray from the Torah or become lax in performing our duties. In His abundant compassion, He gives us repeated chances to do *teshuvah* (repent), and when we do, He accepts us with open arms, so to speak.

Even when we sin, God continues to act benevolently toward us. He looks beyond our misdemeanors to our true essence, our underlying wish to come close to Him, to worship Him with all our might, with all our desire, and with all our soul. And God is patient. He knows that there is goodness in each of us, for He has created us with a *neshamah* (soul), a part of God Himself, which enables us to attain the greatest spiritual heights. He has given us the Torah and mitzvos to guide us and refine our character so that we can, as it were, climb up Yaakov's ladder, one rung at a time, looking upward before each step we take in life, asking ourselves, "How does God want me to act at this given moment in time?"

Why do I mention Yaakov's ladder? In Yaakov Avinu's famous dream, angels were going up and down the ladder and God Himself was at the top. As we climb our own spiritual ladder, we can close our eyes for a moment and imagine that angels are helping us come closer to God. We should feel grateful that He permits us mortal beings to come close to Him. Our rabbis teach that there is no greater enjoyment than to be *davuk baHashem* (deeply connected to God). This is what happens in Gan Eden. We experience different degrees of *deveikus* (closeness to God), commensurate with how much we have elevated ourselves spiritually.

Our primary goal on this earth is to give thanks to the Creator. This idea is expressed by the Men of the Great Assembly, who formulated our prayers:

> It is the obligation of all creatures to give thanks, to praise, to laud, to glorify, to extol, to honor, to bless, to exalt, and acclaim You, even beyond all the words of song and adoration of David the son of Yishai, Your anointed servant.[24]

---

24   *Nishmas* prayer.

Notice the richness of the vocabulary. When it comes to praising God, no matter how many expressions of praise we utter, we can never adequately praise the Almighty Creator.

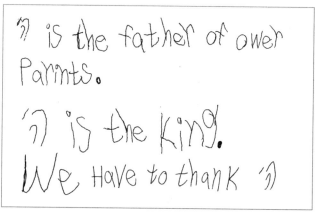

Kaylee, age 5

THE JEWISH CALENDAR

If we take a look at the Jewish calendar, we see that the theme of *hakaras hatov* runs through all our holidays.

Pesach is the festival when we express our gratitude to God for freeing us from slavery and taking us out of Egypt. We enumerate the many miracles He performed for us, both in Egypt and at the splitting of the Yam Suf (Sea of Reeds).

Shavuos is the festival when we express our gratitude for receiving the Torah and becoming God's Chosen People. Also, it is the season of the first fruits, for which we are abundantly grateful.

Sukkos is the festival when we thank God for the Clouds of Glory that accompanied us for forty years in the wilderness. It is also the season of the harvesting of the crops, a time of great joy.

Rosh Hashanah is the festival when we acknowledge that God is our King and the King of the entire universe. We remind ourselves of the very special relationship we have with Him, for which we should be abundantly thankful.

On **Yom Kippur**, God forgives us our transgressions, provided we have made amends. Shouldn't we be thankful for this?

On **Purim** we thank God for saving us from physical annihilation, and on **Chanukah** we give thanks to Him for delivering us from the threat of being cut off from our religion.

On **Tu B'Shevat**, the birthday of the trees, we thank God for the multiple blessings we derive from trees: for their fruits, their beauty, and if we think about it, the shade they provide in the hot summer months and for purifying the air that we breathe. On this festival, it is the custom in my family and in others to eat fifteen different kinds of fruit that grow on trees and to recite the fifteen psalms of *Shir Hamaalos* (fifteen songs of praise to the Creator),[25] one after each fruit.

SEDER NIGHT

What is the reason for the mitzvah of *Maggid*, talking about the Exodus from Egypt? This commandment is given to us so that we will arouse in ourselves limitless feelings of gratitude to God. The more we talk about the miracles and the more we feel that we were actually slaves and that we were redeemed, the more grateful we become.

We are told that whoever speaks at length about our going out of Egypt is to be praised. This is the only mitzvah where we are specifically told that the more we engage ourselves in it, the more praiseworthy we are. I understand this to mean that the more gratitude we have to God, the more we are to be praised. Seemingly, there is no limit to how much gratitude we need to have to God.

The mitzvah of matzah and the mitzvah of *maror* (bitter herbs) is to eat a *k'zayis* (a quantity equaling the volume of an olive). The mitzvah of *Maggid*, talking about the Exodus and feeling grateful, is not limited to a specific amount; on the contrary, the more gratitude we feel, the more credit we get. That's also the reason why we recite *Hallel* at the Seder (it's the only time we say *Hallel* at night)—because in *Hallel*, we recount God's miracles, and thank Him for them. Singing praise to God stems from feelings of deep gratitude.

A popular song that we sing at the Seder is *Dayeinu*. It lists fifteen gifts of God for which the Jewish nation is grateful. We owe thanks for

---

25   *Tehillim* (Psalms) 120–134.

each and every one of these gifts. Had God taken us out from Egypt but not executed judgments upon the Egyptians, we sing, "It would have been enough." Had He given us Shabbos but not brought us to Har Sinai, we sing, "It would have been enough." Had He given us the Torah but not led us into the Land of Israel, again we sing, "It would have been enough." The song concludes with:

> *How much more are we indebted for the multitude of bounties which God has bestowed upon us. He took us out from Egypt, executed judgment upon the Egyptians and their gods, slew their firstborn, gave us their wealth, divided the sea for us, caused us to pass through its midst on dry land, drowned our oppressors in the sea, supplied us with everything for forty years, fed us with manna, gave us Shabbos, brought us to Har Sinai, gave us the Torah, brought us to the Land of Israel, and built the Beis Hamikdash for us to atone for all our iniquities.*

Indeed, both as a nation and as individuals, we are deeply indebted to God.

WHAT ARE YOU GRATEFUL FOR?

You may think that practicing gratitude is something only spiritually minded people do, but in truth, everyday people are often filled with the grace and energy of gratitude. Many people have a wonderful, positive, gratitude-attitude to life.

> "I wake up grateful every day. I'm alive. Another day!"
>
> *Secretary*

> "I'm grateful that I'm living. If I pass away, that's what God wants."
>
> *Blind woman I met on a bus, case manager*

> "I'm grateful that with faith and belief in myself, I can accomplish anything. It's gratitude that lets you enjoy life."
>
> *Car service driver*

"I have gratitude to God that I have received life and have all the possible tools to make this life valuable and happy, if we follow the rules of the Ten Commandments and we know that we have free will to choose the right thing."

Colette Aboulker Muscat, my mentor from Jerusalem
with whom I studied for twenty-three years[26]

"For me, gratitude is an overwhelming feeling of thank you and love, particularly for the natural world; that seems to be the greatest happiness for me. When I'm in nature, it makes me feel alive. If I go where the trees are, I feel grateful. Trees are just there; they never argue with you. I am exceedingly grateful for them and for carrots and for water.

Ask yourself what gratitude looks like, sounds like, tastes like, smells like. For me, it's an apple pie, a baby after a bath."

Denise, my poetry-writing friend[27]

IMAGERY EXERCISES TO INCREASE OUR GRATITUDE TO GOD

God has endowed us with so many blessings: the ability to see, hear, smell, touch, and taste; the ability to talk, walk, think, learn, be creative, communicate, relate to others, procreate. One of the greatest gifts God has given us is the ability to exercise free choice. And, of course, we owe our very lives to God. It's easy to take these things for granted. We

---

26 Colette was born in 1909 in Algeria to an illustrious family descended from the Ben Ish Chai. Her father, a noted neurosurgeon in Europe, was also a communal leader. Colette dedicated her life to teaching and healing the hundreds of students who flocked to her from all parts of the world. A favorite saying of hers was, "You're not here to have a good time, you're here to reach truth, to reach spirit." In 1995, Colette was awarded the annual citizen prize, Yakir Yerushalayim (Worthy Citizen of Jerusalem), inaugurated in 1967, in recognition of her outstanding contribution. She died peacefully in her home in November of 2003. She was ninety-four years old.

27 Denise and I met at a writing conference in the summer of 1998 and remained friends until her demise from Alzheimer's in 2017. She was exceptionally loving, generous, and kind— a treasure in my life. For years she sent me cards four times annually: for Rosh Hashanah, Chanukah, Pesach, and my birthday.

need to stop periodically and take stock, recognize all these blessings for what they are and bless God.

The exercises that follow will help us more fully realize the enormity of our debt of gratitude to God so that we don't fall into the trap of taking His gifts for granted. They take no more than two minutes, some a mere few seconds, because change takes place in an instant. They are a powerful way to get in touch with feelings, gain insights, and effect change. It is important at the outset to have the right *kavanah* (intention, direction, and will). You may want somebody to read the exercises to you. You can also record them and listen to the recording or read them in this book. It is good to do an exercise three times a day: in the morning, while still in bed; in the afternoon, before eating your lunch; and in the evening in bed, before falling asleep. Keeping to a routine will help keep you from forgetting. See whether you can do an exercise a day and notice how you are becoming happier and enjoying enhanced relationships. See also how the exercises deepen your relationship with God. If you have the right intention and the will to become a more grateful person, you will surely succeed!

When doing an exercise, it is a good idea to have a special book handy in which you write and draw your responses, preferably in the colors you see in your images. Use the present tense to keep the images alive; say, "I see..." rather than "I saw..." and, "I hear..." rather than "I heard..."

To do these exercises in an optimal manner, find a quiet place where you will not be disturbed. Sit comfortably in your chair, hands resting on your thighs, legs uncrossed. At the conclusion of each exercise, breathe out once and open your eyes.

Induction (to be done before every exercise): Close your eyes. Breathe out slowly through your mouth three times, and:

- See how you are shining your unique, specific talents and giftedness into the world and thank God for endowing you with these special qualities.
- See yourself creating a personal prayer of thanksgiving to God.

  - Imagine you are writing this prayer on an imaginary screen in your head.

- Read aloud what you have written, then concretely write this prayer on a piece of paper. (Suggestion: Keep this prayer with you wherever you go. It will serve as a reminder to be grateful to God for the multiple Divine blessings of which you are the recipient on a daily basis.)
- Hear yourself thanking God, not only for the bounty you have received so far in your life, but also for the things you wish to have or attain in the future.
  - Thank God as if you already have been granted these things.
  - See, feel, sense, and know how doing this helps manifest these things concretely in your life.
- Imagine you are composing a song of gratitude to God.
  - Hear the melody in your mind.
- See how, when you are grateful to God, you are connecting yourself to the Source of all good.
- Identify one of your character traits that you wish to improve and perfect.
  - See how you are accomplishing this and thank God for giving you the insight, the motivation, the creativity, and the steadfastness to succeed.
- See, sense, and know how the commandment to remember the Revelation at Sinai is reason to have gratitude to the Creator.
  - Hear yourself singing His praises, together with the angels.
  - Imagine you are an angel singing praise to God.
- See how the more we appreciate the world God created, the more gratitude we can feel for the Creator.
  - See, sense, and know how the more gratitude we have for the Creator, the more we come to love Him and the more things to be grateful for will show up in our lives.
- See the different ways you are creating your home to be a holy sanctuary.
  - Sense God's Presence in the home you have created.

Gratitude Practices

- Meditate on the idea that "God is glad I'm here," or use this as an affirmation that you write down many times and repeatedly say to yourself. Make this a daily practice.
- Start your day reciting the *Modeh Ani* prayer. Really try to focus on the words.
- Go out and enjoy nature as often as you can. Your world will be richer for it.
- Take up gardening or, if you have no garden, grow plants indoors. It is exciting to witness bulbs bringing forth tulips or watch a miniature rosebush blossom right in your living room. Or treat yourself by buying an orchid and enjoying its beauty for months on end.
- Practice reading from *Sefer Tehillim* (King David's psalms of song and praise) for five minutes a day. If this is too much, do it for three minutes, and if this is too much, do it for two minutes or even one minute. Begin at the beginning of the book and work your way through, starting each day where you left off the previous day until you reach the very end. Then begin again.
- In addition to reciting *Tehillim*, you might compose a personal book of thanksgiving that you could recite during a specific time of day. You could make this a ritual, knowing that the greatest language of praise is thanksgiving because it flows directly from the soul, the uppermost element of man.

CHAPTER 3

How Much Is Enough?

*Train yourself never to put off the word
or action for the expression of gratitude.*

Albert Schweitzer

*Getting a drop of water, giving back
a spring...*

Chinese aphorism[1]

IT IS A MITZVAH to remember the kindnesses and wonders God performed for us in Egypt and the wilderness. We do this twice every day, morning and evening, so there will be no chance of us ever forgetting it.

While it is not a commandment to have *hakaras hatov* to the Egyptians who tortured our ancestors with backbreaking forced labor for 210 years, we accept them should they wish to convert. Children born to them can be admitted to the congregation of Hashem in the third generation; that is to say, they are even allowed to marry us after three generations. The rationale for this is that we have to appreciate that they allowed us to live in their land during Yosef's reign.[2]

One of the reasons people fail to express gratitude is because they forget the good others have done for them. In order to be grateful, we have to remember. But why must we remember for such a long time? Because

---

1   A grateful person should repay hundredfold or thousandfold. Hong Zicheng, *Cai-Gen-Tan* (Chinese classic text on human relationships), c. 1590.

2   *Devarim* (Deuteronomy) 23:8–9.

remembering engenders feelings of gratitude within us and teaches us that we have to have *hakaras hatov* not only to people from whom we benefited today or yesterday, or even last week or last month or a year ago; we have to have gratitude to people from whom we benefited five, ten, twenty years ago—and well beyond that. We must continue to have gratitude to anyone who has *ever* helped us in our lives, no matter how long ago it happened. We must never forget a kindness shown to us.

WHAT HAVE YOU DONE FOR ME LATELY?

> *A congressman solicited a constituent's vote and learned that the man planned to vote for his opponent.*
>
> *"How can you do that?" the congressman objected. "Don't you remember that time ten years ago when your business burned down, and I arranged for you to get a low-interest loan from the Small Business Administration? And what about the time your daughter got in trouble with the police overseas, and I arranged for her to be released and sent back to the United States? And the time when your wife was sick, and I helped get her admitted to the special hospital she needed?"*
>
> *The voter answered, "That's all true…but what have you done for me lately?"*

Every joke has a kernel of truth. "What have you done for me lately?" is the ingrate's question. Judaism's perspective is quite different.

FROM GENERATION TO GENERATION

In *Sefer Melachim* we read that on his deathbed, King David instructed his son and successor, Solomon, and reminded him to "show kindness to the sons of Barzillai of Gilad, and let them be of those that eat at your table, for they befriended me [many years ago] when I fled from Avshalom your brother."[3] King David thus sought to perpetuate his gratitude into the next generation.

---

3   *Melachim I* (I Kings) 2:7.

In contemporary times, Rabbi Joseph Soloveitchik, affectionately known as "the Rav" to his students, exhibited exceptional gratitude for any favor done to his family. Over several months he traveled from Manhattan to the Bronx every Wednesday to visit a woman undergoing chemotherapy. Her only connection to the Rav was that her father had done a kindness for Rabbi Soloveitchik's father, Reb Moshe.

When Dr. Louis Ginsberg died, the Rav went to visit the grieving family during shivah. The surprised mourners asked him if he knew Dr. Ginsberg. Rabbi Soloveitchik replied that he had met him only once, when Professor Ginsberg had paid a shivah call following the death of the Rav's father.

NOTHING TOO SMALL

We may be under the mistaken impression that gratitude need only be expressed when receiving a large favor or something of great value. This is erroneous. We need to show appreciation for the smallest benefits we derive from another person, regardless of whether the benefactor intended to benefit us, regardless of whether he made a big effort, and regardless of whether it cost the benefactor money. So long as we derive even some minuscule benefit, it is incumbent upon us to feel appreciation and express thanks.

It is mentioned in the Talmud that somebody removed a feather from the hat of the sage known as Ameimar. This rabbi, who was a judge, recused himself from adjudicating the case of the man who removed the feather lest he might favor him due to the gratitude he felt on account of the benefit he received from that slight assistance.[4]

The Talmud further tells us about the Amora Shmuel, who was having difficulty crossing a rickety footbridge. Someone helped him cross the bridge, and it turned out that this individual had a court case scheduled to be heard in Shmuel's court. Shmuel disqualified himself from judging the case, fearing he might not be completely impartial due to

---

4   *Kesubos* 105b.

the possibility of feeling favorably disposed toward the man who had helped him.[5]

A similar Talmudic anecdote concerns the judge Rabbi Yishmael, who rented out his garden. Every Friday, according to the terms of the rental agreement, the renter brought Rabbi Yishmael a basket of fruit. Once, the tenant delivered the fruit on Thursday. When Rabbi Yishmael asked him why, he replied, "I have a lawsuit and I thought that while I was on my way here, I would bring the fruit to you." Rabbi Yishmael did not accept it, saying, "I am disqualified from being your judge."[6]

Polish-born Torah scholar Rabbi Simcha Sheps[7] escaped the Holocaust by traveling through Siberia and Japan. He ultimately joined the faculty of Torah Vodaath in New York. Along with his erudition and love for his students, he was known for his trait of *hakaras hatov*, acknowledging the good done for him by others. He insisted on attending the funeral of a Chassidic Rebbe with whom he had no particular connection, only because he had once refreshed himself in the air-conditioned lobby of the Rebbe's *beis midrash* (study hall)!

The Rosh Yeshiva's Plants

Our debt of gratitude is not limited to humans; it extends to anything from which we have derived benefit, as seen in the following story about Rabbi Yisroel Gustman.

As a young man, barely eighteen years old, Rabbi Gustman had been a *dayan* (judge) in Vilna in Rabbi Chaim Ozer Grodzinski's *beis din* (rabbinical court). After World War II, he was Rosh Yeshiva of Netzach Yisroel in Brooklyn, and subsequently in Jerusalem.

Can you imagine this Torah giant watering the plants in front of the yeshiva building? The *talmidim* (Torah students) who passed by were shocked to see the Rosh Yeshiva performing such menial work. They urged him to let them take over, but Rabbi Gustman refused.

---

5   Ibid.
6   Ibid.
7   1908 (or 1911)–1998

"My life was saved by the shrubs I ate in the forest while I was hiding from the Nazis. I feel obligated to show my appreciation for the plants that saved my life; therefore, I insist on watering the plants personally, to show my gratitude."

Grateful Goodbyes

Whenever Rabbi Menachem Mendel of Kotzk replaced a pair of worn-out shoes, he would neatly wrap the old ones in newspaper before placing them in the trash.

"How can I simply toss away such a fine pair of shoes that have served me so well these past years?" he would ask.

Similarly, I've heard it said that when Rabbi Mordechai Schwab's suit became frayed, he wrapped it up and kept the package for a few days before disposing of it.[8] Then he would say, *"Du hast mir gut badint—*You served me well."

I Must Clean It Myself!

The great Mussar teacher Rabbi Elya Lopian was talking to a student while folding his prayer shawl. The tallis was large and he had to rest it on a nearby bench. After he finished, Reb Elya noticed that the bench was dusty.

"I need to find a towel to clean the bench," he said. His student ran to get the towel, but Reb Elya would not allow him to wipe the bench.

"No! No!" he said, holding up his hand. "I must clean it myself! I must show gratitude to the bench upon which I folded my tallis."

NEVER TOO LATE

If we can be grateful to inanimate objects like shoes, benches, and clothing, how much more so do we need to appreciate human beings, who have free will and help us consciously, out of the goodness of their hearts? How much effort do we make to thank the people who have helped us? Do we try to remember those who have helped us in

---

8   Rabbi Mordechai Schwab was the *Mashgiach* of Beis Shraga in Monsey, NY.

the past? Do we take the trouble to locate them and express our thanks? How many years do we go back?

Schindler's List

Some people search for a lifetime in order to express gratitude for a benefit they received many years—even decades—before.

Leopold ("Poldek") Pfefferberg was one of the 1,100 Jews saved by Oskar Schindler during World War II. His heart was full of thankfulness and he vowed to make Schindler's name known throughout the world. But it wasn't as easy as he had thought. Nonetheless, he never gave up.

In 1950, he moved to Los Angeles, where he opened a leather goods store. Actors and actresses from Hollywood patronized his shop. He never missed an opportunity to talk to them about how he and hundreds of others had been saved by Schindler. He was hoping that one of the film stars would make a film depicting Schindler's heroic story, but no one was interested.

One day, the wife of a prominent movie producer brought in two expensive handbags for repair. Pfefferberg told her that if she allowed him to speak to her husband, he wouldn't charge her a penny. She agreed, the husband came, and Pfefferberg told him about Schindler. Intrigued, the producer wrote a film about him—but no studio was interested in making it.

Pfefferberg remained undaunted. Throughout the 1960s and '70s, he continued to tell Schindler's story to whomever he met.

In October 1980, Australian novelist Thomas Keneally walked into Pfefferberg's store to purchase a briefcase. Pfefferberg told him about Schindler, and how he had saved 1,100 Jews from certain death at the hands of the Nazis. When he learned that Keneally was an author, he urged him to write a book recounting Schindler's story. Intrigued, Keneally said the story was worthy of being told, but "I am not the person to write it. I was only three years old when the war broke out and don't know too much about it. Moreover," he added, "I am a Catholic and don't know much about what happened to the Jews during the Holocaust, and am not knowledgeable about Jewish suffering."

Pfefferberg wouldn't take no for an answer. Thirty-three years had passed since he'd made his vow to Schindler, who was now deceased. He was determined to keep his promise. "I lived through it," he said, "and will tell you everything I know. With a little research, you will be as educated as anybody about this period in history. As an Irish Catholic and notable author, you will have more credibility, not less, in writing about the Holocaust.

"You say you know nothing about Jewish suffering. Irish people have suffered for four hundred years, and human suffering is the same whether Jewish or Irish."

After hearing Pfefferberg's words, Keneally committed himself to writing the book. In 1982, *Schindler's Ark* was published and earned international acclaim. In 1993, Steven Spielberg's film *Schindler's List*, based on Keneally's book, was released and later won seven Academy Awards. The promise a grateful Pfefferberg had made to Oskar Schindler in 1947 had finally been fulfilled.

Royal Gratitude
THE RABBI'S BLESSING

When Queen Wilhelmina of Holland traveled to Marienbad in 1908, a tremendous crowd was waiting at the station when she and her entourage arrived. Inquiries yielded the information that a Chassidic rabbi had just arrived as well and these people were his followers.

The queen was deeply religious and knew what a rabbi was, but the concept of a Chassidic one was unfamiliar. "People come from far and wide," she was told, "to get advice and blessings from this holy man."

At that time, the succession of the Dutch monarchy was in jeopardy. Queen Wilhelmina's three half-brothers had died, and she herself was childless. Doctors had told her there was no likelihood she would ever bear a child.

The queen decided to ask the rabbi for a blessing. She sent a message asking him to see her, and they arranged to meet in a beautiful park in Marienbad.

When Queen Wilhelmina saw the Munkatcher Rebbe, she immediately perceived his holiness. Her tears began to flow as she confided her worry that the Dutch monarchy would come to an end due to her apparent infertility.

The Rebbe instructed his interpreter, "Tell the queen that within a year she will give birth to a child and her kingdom will last until the Messiah comes."

The following year, Queen Wilhelmina gave birth to a daughter, whom she named Juliana.

THE QUEEN REMEMBERS

More than three decades later, during World War II, a righteous person named Rabbi Yaakov Tzvi Katz was deported to the Bergen-Belsen concentration camp and his eighteen-year-old son was killed. The Nazis confiscated twelve holy books he had carried with him, ripped them apart, and burned them. After the war, he wanted to return home to Hungary but nothing was left there for him.

Many Jews thought Holland would be a place where survivors could rebuild their shattered lives. Rabbi Katz wrote to the Dutch immigration department and applied for a visa. On the application, he listed his profession as "rabbi." In due time, he received a rejection letter. Holland had no need for rabbis, he was told. They only wanted people who could contribute economically to the country.

In desperation, Rabbi Katz penned a letter in Yiddish to Queen Wilhelmina. After the proper salutations, he wrote: "You surely remember that you went to Marienbad in 1908 and, while there, you received a blessing from the Munkatcher Rabbi. I was the person who interpreted the rabbi's blessing to you. As a show of gratitude for this, I am asking you to please help me get a visa to settle in your country."

Upon reading his letter, the queen overruled the immigration department and Rabbi Katz was subsequently welcomed to Holland.

During his tenure as a rabbi, he authored a book. In the introduction, Rabbi Katz stated: "I have tremendous gratitude to Queen Wilhelmina and I give her a blessing that her monarchy should endure." Princess Juliana ascended to the throne in 1948. She had four daughters and was succeeded by the eldest of them, Beatrix, who, in turn, had three sons. The eldest, Willem-Alexander, has become the country's first king since 1890. He has three lovely young daughters and the Dutch monarchy remains secure to this day.

Time and Effort

On August 7, 1945, in a daring rescue, US paratroopers liberated the 1,400 Americans and other nationals held prisoner by the Japanese during World War II. Forty years later, in 1985, one of the former captives, a woman who was twelve years old at the time of the rescue, took action. She obtained a US government document, which had, by then, been declassified, listing the names of the seven men who took part in the mission. With years of effort she located all the men (by then in their seventies) who were still alive, and the widows of those who had passed away, in order to express her gratitude.

"It's never too late to say thank you," she said.

Rav Shach Gives Thanks

WARM FEELINGS

When he was already old, sickly, and very feeble, Rav Shach, one of the great Torah scions of the twentieth century, traveled to Haifa during a storm to attend the funeral of a simple woman. Nobody could comprehend why he inconvenienced himself to this extent. Finally, someone asked him to explain.

He described how when he was a young *yeshiva bachur* (student), he often went without food, but worse than the gnawing hunger was the excruciating cold. During the day, he said, it was tolerable because he steeped himself in learning, but the nights were unbearable. It had reached the point that he was thinking of leaving yeshiva and accepting his uncle's offer to go into business with him.

One day, a woman gave him a blanket. That night, he was able to sleep.

"I was so warm that Friday night that I changed my mind and decided to stay. This lady is the person who just died, so I felt obliged to attend her funeral out of deep gratitude for what she had done for me so many decades ago."

NOT ONE MOMENT LONGER

It happened once that a certain person came to visit Rav Shach. When the Rosh Yeshiva heard the name of the man's father, he inquired as to his whereabouts. The visitor told him his father was in the Tamir, a senior citizens' home in Jerusalem. "I must visit him right away!" Rav Shach exclaimed.

His visitor was puzzled. Why did the *Gadol Hador* (Torah giant of the generation) feel the need to hasten to his father's side? Rav Shach explained that when he was a young and unknown rabbi, hardly anyone came to his *shiurim* (Torah classes). This man's father was one of the few who used to attend the rabbi's classes.

"By attending my *shiurim*," said Rav Shach, "your father gave me encouragement to continue. All my life I wished I could thank him for his support. Now that I have the opportunity to do so, I don't want to wait even one more minute!"[9]

RULES OF THE GAME

On a thank-you visit, Rav Shach brought along a toy for the children of the person to whom he wished to express gratitude. He met with their father and then sat with the children, teaching them how to play. Only when he saw that they had grasped the objectives and rules of the game did he leave to go home.

This was a leading Torah giant who used every minute to learn and teach Torah! Clearly, he considered taking time out of his busy schedule to play with the children of someone from whom he had benefited, to be what the Torah expects of us.

A Timely Invitation

Rabbi Isser Zalman Meltzer, the prominent Rosh Yeshiva and Torah scholar, and father-in-law of Rabbi Aharon Kotler, was invited by a former student to a reception in honor of the bar mitzvah of his son. The student did not expect him to attend as they lived far away from the elderly rabbi, in a fourth floor walk-up, and it was a scorching hot summer's day.

---

9   I heard this story from my nephew Adam Murciano, in Israel.

Imagine the student's surprise when he saw Rabbi Isser Zalman struggling up the four flights of stairs, perspiring profusely and stopping to catch his breath every few steps!

"I didn't expect the Rabbi to come. It's so hot and so far away," the student said contritely.

Rabbi Isser Zalman replied, "I came because of *hakaras hatov*. I owe you a debt of gratitude and I came to show my appreciation."

The student was puzzled. Rabbi Isser Zalman explained. "I happened to be present at your son's *bris* (circumcision). When I received your invitation, I realized how much time had elapsed. A student of mine is making a bar mitzvah for his son! I realized I was getting old and it's time for me to do *teshuvah* (atone). So I owe you a debt of gratitude."

Giving Back

A doctor in Shaare Zedek Hospital in Jerusalem works with prematurely born babies. He himself had been a preemie.

"Taking care of these tiny infants is my way of giving back. It's my way of saying thank you to those doctors and nurses who took care of me at my birth," he explained.

Meisei Mitzvah

A woman was tragically hit by a car in B'nei Brak. Chapters of *Tehillim* were immediately recited in many synagogues, but, sadly, she succumbed to her injuries and passed away. The *chevrah kadisha* (burial society) tried to find out the woman's identity. They looked in her handbag and found out that she lived in Holon. They called the house, but no one answered, so they called a number of people in Holon who investigated and found out that the woman lived alone and had no known family.

The police wanted to do an autopsy, but the *chevrah kadisha* implored them to desist since it is against the Jewish religion. Amazingly, the police allowed the woman to be buried intact.

Loudspeakers mounted on cars blared the news throughout the city that there would be a funeral that afternoon for Ms. Schwartz,[10] a *meis*

---

10   A fictitious name.

mitzvah (deceased person who has no next of kin). A huge crowd of men and women came to pay their respects. The woman was buried, *Tehillim* was recited, and the mourners dispersed.

Suddenly, a woman was seen approaching from the opposite direction, proceeding toward the freshly covered grave. A man asked if he could help her. She said she was heading to the grave of the woman who had just been buried.

"Did you know the deceased?" the man inquired.

"We met a long time ago in the Warsaw ghetto," she said. "Food was scarce and children died in the streets from starvation every day. It was extremely dangerous to go out to bury them. But this woman who was just buried risked her life to bury some of my siblings. I just wanted to say thank you."

THANKING OUR TEACHERS

Think where you would be today if you had not had teachers, if you had not been taught to read or write. You'd have been denied the world of books, of ideas, of wisdom, of knowledge. Perhaps each one of us should sit down now and compose a letter of appreciation to our first-grade teacher or the teacher(s) who inspired us the most, thanking them for expanding our minds and hearts, and for enriching our lives beyond measure.

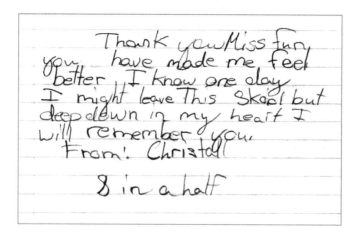

The following is a beautiful letter written by Albert Camus to his childhood teacher after he received the Nobel Prize for Literature.

19 November 1957

Dear Monsieur Germain,

I let the commotion around me these days subside a bit before speaking to you from the bottom of my heart. I have just been given far too great an honor, one I neither sought nor solicited.

But when I heard the news, my first thought, after my mother, was of you. Without you, without the affectionate hand you extended to the small poor child that I was, without your teaching and example, none of all this would have happened.

I don't make too much of this sort of honor. But at least it gives me the opportunity to tell you what you have been and still are for me, and to assure you that your efforts, your work, and the generous heart you put into it still live in one of your little schoolboys who, despite the years, has never stopped being your grateful pupil. I embrace you with all my heart.

Albert Camus

Ancient History

Esther's[11] history teacher had made a great impact on her. Under his tutelage, she developed an abiding love for the subject, which she now taught in high school. It occurred to her that she had never thanked him for inculcating in her such a love for learning and teaching history. So she emailed him a letter of gratitude, expressing her deep-felt appreciation, telling him how he had changed her life and given her hours upon hours of enjoyment.

What Esther did not know at the time was that this teacher had moved to Israel and was having difficulties adjusting to a new country and, particularly, with disciplining students. Disheartened and deeply discouraged, he had decided to leave the teaching profession—but didn't yet know how else to support himself and his family.

When he received Esther's email letting him know what a fabulous teacher he was and how he was able to enrich the lives of his pupils, he changed his mind and continued teaching. He eventually adapted to Israel's ways and went on to inspire hundreds of other students in his new homeland.

Nourishing Both Body and Soul

The teacher of a fifth-grade class noticed that one of her students looked scrawny and unkempt. His mother had died and he lived with his sister, who had a baby to feed. There wasn't enough food to go around.

---

11   A fictitious name.

Every day the teacher brought the boy two meals, one for breakfast and one for lunch.

Years passed. The teacher's mother, who had lived in a nursing home for twenty years, died at the age of one hundred, and her death announcement appeared in a newspaper. Among the letters of condolence was one from this orphan boy.

"You will have forgotten me," he wrote, "but I will never forget you. I am a happy family man with a wife and three children. I'm a lawyer. Thank you for all those meals you gave me forty-nine years ago when I was in fifth grade. Thank you for taking a great part in helping me make something of myself, helping me become the person I am."[12]

Gratitude Practices

- Pick one person each week, or each month, and write a letter (not an email, which is impersonal and mechanical) telling them how they helped you. Be specific and say thank you in the best way you know how. It could be a child or an adult, a teacher, family member, friend, rabbi, colleague, or neighbor.
- Visit a teacher from your elementary school and share with them how they inspired you, gave you a love for a specific subject, enabled you to have a better life. Give as many details as you can think of.
- Do the same for a high school teacher.
- Keep a small stone or a crystal in your pocket. Whenever you put your hand in your pocket and touch it, think of someone or something from whom you've benefited. Thank them in your heart and wish them well.

12 This story was told to me by my friend Ora Baer, who knew the teacher.

CHAPTER 4

Gratitude in Adversity

He is a wise man who does not grieve for the things which he has not, but rejoices for those which he has.

Epictetus

Both abundance and lack exist simultaneously in our lives, as parallel realities. When we choose not to focus on what is missing from our lives but are grateful for the abundance...the wasteland of illusion falls away and we experience Heaven on earth.

Sarah ban Breathnach

He who lived in concentration camps can remember the men who walked through the huts comforting others, giving away their last piece of bread. They may have been few in number but they offer sufficient proof that everything can be taken from a man but one thing: the last of the human freedoms—to choose one's attitude in any given set of circumstances.

Viktor Frankl[1]

---

1   *Man's Search for Meaning*, p. 86 (Beacon, 1946). Frankl was a Viennese psychiatrist who survived the Nazi concentration camps but lost his wife in the Holocaust.

HAIR DOS AND DON'TS

A woman woke up in the morning, looked in the mirror, and saw that she had three hairs on her head.

"Oh, good," she said, "I think I'll braid my hair today." And she did and had a wonderful day.

The next morning, she looked in the mirror and saw that she had two hairs on her head. "Today I'll part my hair!" she exclaimed, and she did and had a fun day.

The next morning, she looked in the mirror and saw that she had only one hair on her head. "Great! Today I'll wear a ponytail," she said, and she had a great day.

The next day she looked in the mirror and saw she had no hairs. "Oh, good," she said. "Today I don't have to fix my hair."

What a lesson for all of us!

ME?!

The story is told of a student who went to his rabbi and said, "Rabbi, I have such a hard life. Teach me how to make peace with it." The rabbi told him to travel to a neighboring village and there, to approach a certain Reb Zusha, who would be able to answer him.

When he got there, he asked the villagers where Reb Zusha lived. They pointed to a humble, dilapidated cottage. As he approached, he saw the roof needed repair and the windows were broken. He entered and saw a sparsely furnished room with only a table and two wobbly chairs. Then he noticed Reb Zusha, clad in a threadbare coat, blisters on his hands.

"My rabbi sent me to you to learn how I can make peace with my lot in life," the student said.

"Me?!" said Reb Zusha in astonishment. "I haven't had a difficult day in my life!"

ALL FOR THE GOOD

We all experience times when we are faced with difficult challenges: loss of a job, health issues, non-compliant or academically failing children, marital strife. It's hard during these times to find it within oneself to feel gratitude. How can we stay calm and even grateful in the face of adversity?

If we have the mindset that Divine love is behind everything that is happening to us, if we become aware that God is the orchestrator of our lives and that everything that happens to us is a manifestation of His will and has a purpose, we may look at adversity with new eyes. We may see it as an opportunity for spiritual growth, making it possible for us to say, "Thanks for helping me remember why I'm here."

Judaism teaches us to bless God for the bad as well as for the good and that in the future there will be only one blessing, *"Ha'tov V'Ha'meitiv—*He is Good and He does good," because at that time we will recognize that everything was really good. Though it may not be easy in the face of adversity to feel that the bad is actually good, having such a perspective affords us opportunities for amazing growth and makes it possible for us to attain incredible spiritual heights.

Sometimes, God denies us something. We are taught that even that is for our good, though we may not always see it as such. Judaism teaches that God gives us whatever we need, and whatever circumstances are necessary, for us to reach the purpose for which we were created and earn *Olam Haba*, a place in the World to Come.[2]

King David is an example of someone whose life was filled with adversity upon adversity. He was shunned by his siblings, then persecuted for years by King Saul, who was bent on killing him. He lost four children in his lifetime. His son Amnon raped his half-sister, David's daughter Tamar, and his son Avshalom raised a formidable army against him in an attempt to overthrow him. Despite these tragic and tumultuous events, the book of *Tehillim*, which he composed, is replete with praises of God. Time and again he says, *"Tov l'hodos laHashem—*It is good to give thanks to the Lord," and he often repeats, *"Ki l'olam chasdo—*For His loving kindness is eternal."

Nor did the proverbial Iyov (Job) complain in the face of his manifold afflictions. Despite losing his seven sons, all his wealth, and even his

---

2   "Every Jewish person has a portion in the World to Come" (*Pirkei Avos, Sanhedrin* 10:1).

health, he remained loyal to God. "You have clothed me in skin and flesh," he declared, "and knit me together with bones and sinews. You have bestowed life and kindness upon me, and Your provisions have spared my spirit."[3]

HIDDEN GOOD

The Talmud describes a man called Nachum Ish Gamzu. No matter what happened, he was able to see it as good. If something seemed adverse, he would say, "*Gam zu l'tovah*—This also is for the best." This amazing man is an example from whom we can learn to improve our faith in God and to strive to see whatever happens with the "good eye" that the rabbis discuss in *Pirkei Avos* (Ethics of the Fathers).[4] This is not easy; it requires a great deal of faith, tenacity, and patience. Every step we take that brings us closer to our goal is of consequence. It's important that we become our own cheerleaders, applaud every step we take in the right direction, and compliment ourselves each time we see improvement.

The Talmud tells us about Rabbi Akiva, who was a poor, ignorant shepherd. Though illiterate, he possessed a burning desire to learn and improve himself. He understood the importance of every step. One day, as he was passing a river, he saw a stone with a hole in its center. He understood that the hole was created by the water, one drop at a time, over the course of many years. He realized he could learn Torah drop by drop, step by step. He started out at the age of forty and ultimately rose to the greatest heights of Torah scholarship—so much so that where there is a dispute among the early rabbis in the Talmud, the law is determined by what Rabbi Akiva held to be correct.

Rabbi Akiva was a student of Nachum Ish Gamzu, and, like him, demonstrated an ability to see the good in everything that happened. On one occasion, he stood together with some Torah scholars at the ruins of the Beis Hamikdash. Suddenly, they saw a fox running over the place of the Holy of Holies. The rabbis began to weep, but Rabbi Akiva laughed.

---

3   *Iyov* (Job) 10:11–12.
4   2:13.

"Why do you laugh?" they inquired.

"I laugh," he said, "because I see that the prophecy of foxes running over the ruins of the Beis Hamikdash has been fulfilled. Just as this prophecy has come true, I know that the prophecy of the rebuilding of the Beis Hamikdash will also come true."

It happened once that Rabbi Akiva was walking through a village. As night fell, nobody offered him hospitality, and he had to spend the night in the neighboring forest. He had three things with him: a rooster, a candle, and a donkey. Hardly had he settled himself when a gust blew out the candle. In his typical manner, he said, "This is for the best." Subsequently, a lion came from behind his tent and devoured his donkey. Again, Rabbi Akiva said, "This is for the best." Shortly thereafter, a ravenous fox appeared and consumed the rooster. Rabbi Akiva still said, "Whatever God does must be for the good."

When daybreak arrived, Rabbi Akiva walked back to the village only to find that a marauding band of robbers had killed the villagers and stolen their money. Had the raiders seen the candle, or heard the donkey braying or the rooster crowing, Rabbi Akiva would have met the same fate as the villagers. God had saved his life by extinguishing his candle and taking his animals. At times, when something appears to be bad, it can actually be the best thing that could happen to us.

GRATITUDE IN THE NEW WORLD

The Pilgrims went through extreme hardships. More than half of those who crossed the Atlantic perished from malnutrition and disease within one year, in their new home. All but three families had dug graves in the rocky soil of New England to bury a husband, wife, or child. They had struggled to farm the land, but the barley they planted did very poorly. Other crops failed altogether. Starvation was rampant.

But they were religious people who were versed in the Bible. They knew that the ancient Israelites thanked God at the end of a successful harvest, and also thanked God for delivering them from their captivity in Egypt, thereby gaining their freedom as a people. And so, the Pilgrims did the same. They thanked God for enough corn to survive the winter and also for God's presence in their lives, for His grace and for His love.

They understood that God is to be thanked and praised when times are good and when times are tough, in adversity as well as in prosperity. Their gratitude was a deep trust that goodness ultimately is to be found even in the face of uncertainty.

HAPPY DESPITE HANDICAPS

I attended a meeting to help raise the public's awareness of the handicapped and to get an understanding of their needs. A wheelchair-bound woman in her forties, who suffered from multiple sclerosis, chaired the meeting. She was full of smiles and exuded love and warmth. It was hard for her to talk. Each word was an effort and her diction wasn't easy to understand, yet she chaired the meeting in a dignified manner. Not an ounce of self-pity, not a trace of anger, not an unspoken "Why me?" Her happiness was contagious and touched me deeply. I asked myself, *How would I have reacted if I were in that situation?*

And then there was the Israeli soldier I heard about, who lost both his legs in battle yet was able to quip, "I'm the same person, just a meter shorter!" If he had complained about his situation, grumbled about his plight, and bemoaned the fact that he'd lost his independence—the ability to come and go as he pleased—we would not have been shocked. Yet, this soldier did not let himself sink into despair. He firmly held the attitude that life is good, even with all its vicissitudes: "I am alive, and that, in and of itself, is good."

Such an attitude is the hallmark of a truly grateful person.

NOT EVERYONE IS SO LUCKY

I have read contemporary accounts of people to whom fate dealt a hard blow and yet were able to feel gratitude in the midst of their misfortune.

In *Tuesdays with Morrie*, a highly inspirational book written by Mitch Albom with poignancy and deep sensitivity, the author describes his relationship with his college professor Morrie, who was smitten with ALS, also known as Lou Gehrig's disease.

Morrie comes out of the doctor's office shaken. He has just been told he has two years to live. At that moment he makes a profound decision:

to make the best of the time he has left. He will not live his last days enshrouded in self-pity. He will live with courage and dignity.

As his muscles atrophy, he becomes wheelchair bound, and needs help to get dressed and go to the bathroom. He cannot do the simple things most of us take for granted, like taking out the garbage, shopping, or breathing on his own. It bothers him that he's so utterly dependent, but he says he's trying to enjoy the process.

"Enjoy the process?" Mitch queries. "Yes," Morrie says, finding humor even in such a devastating situation, "after all I get to be a baby one more time."

Morrie could wallow in self-pity, but he refuses to allow his condition to deter him from thinking about what's important in life: to learn to give out love and let it come in; to be as concerned about someone else's situation as you are about your own.

He asks Mitch whether he is giving to his community, whether he's attempting to be fully human. He explains that loving others is the way to find meaning and purpose in life. We are brainwashed into thinking that owning things—more property, more money, and more power—is good, yet we don't get satisfaction from those things, he points out.

"I'm dying," says Morrie. "Devoting myself to loving others is what makes me feel alive. If I can make someone smile after they were feeling sad, it's as close to healthy as I ever feel."

Mitch asks Morrie whether he ever feels sorry for himself. Morrie says he gives himself a good cry in the morning, if he feels he needs to, but then he concentrates on all the good things still in his life, the people who are going to visit, the stories he's going to hear.

As they talk, Mitch notices a pile of newspapers next to Morrie. He expresses surprise that Morrie reads them and wants to keep up with the news; that despite his own suffering and pain he is able to empathize with people around the world suffering from political upheaval—people he doesn't even know. To this, Morrie replies, "Do you think because I'm dying I shouldn't care about what happens in the world?" And then he adds, "It's horrible to watch my body slowly wilt away to nothing. But it's also wonderful because of all the time I get to say goodbye. Not everyone is so lucky."

You might think that someone in his situation would be bitter, angry, and envious, at least much of the time. But here is a man who has shown us that it is possible to live with gratitude and grace, even in the direst of situations.

Read *Tuesdays with Morrie* and learn from his example.

A CHOICE TO BE GRATEFUL

Popular actor Michael J. Fox was stricken with Parkinson's disease in 1991, when he was only twenty-nine years old. Frequently in discomfort and pain, he was interviewed by Emma Brockes of *The Guardian*, US edition, who asked him about the impact of Parkinson's on his life. Without a moment's hesitation, he replied, "I'm grateful for it."

He has written three books: *Lucky Man: A Memoir,*[5] *Always Looking Up: The Adventures of an Incurable Optimist,*[6] and *A Funny Thing Happened: Twists and Turns and Lessons Learned.*[7] In them, he reveals how much the illness has taught him about life and about himself and others, and how grateful he was that he was able to use his fame and resources to increase the public's awareness of the disease and to make a positive difference for those who suffer from it.

He admits he was "freaked out" and took to drinking when he got the diagnosis. He went through a period of seeing himself as he thought others saw him: "Peculiar. Funny looking. [Parkinson's] makes me squirm and it makes my pants ride up so my socks are showing and my shoes fall off, and I can't get the food up to my mouth when I want to." But after years of intense psychotherapy, he changed his views of how the disease affected him.

"I don't care if I don't get food in my mouth. I'm still happy. If my pants are round my ankles, I'm happy. The one choice I don't have is whether or not I have it. But beyond that my choices are infinite. How I approach it is up to me. It has a lot to do with accepting it. And that doesn't mean being resigned or not looking for a cure." He is at such an

---

5   Hyperion Books. 2002.
6   Hyperion Books, 2009.
7   Hachette Books, 2010.

advanced stage of acceptance that he calls the disease "a gift." He is an example of relentless brightness in the face of adversity.

Michael could have remained angry and depressed at the cruel blow fate had dealt him. Instead, he took steps in an effort to eliminate the disease. Toward this end, he created The Michael J. Fox Foundation for Parkinson's Research to benefit millions of people suffering from the disease. His work led him to be named one of the hundred people "whose power, talent, or moral example is transforming the world," in 2007 by *Time* magazine, for his contribution to research in Parkinson's disease.

Michael chose gratitude as a response, teaching us that no matter what our circumstances, we have the choice to be grateful.

THE BEST YEARS OF HIS LIFE

At the age of fifty-seven, Rahamim Melamed-Cohen was happily married with six children and had a highly successful career. He had worked his way up from being a junior high school teacher to becoming superintendent of special education in Jerusalem. He had authored numerous articles on education as well as two books, and he lectured widely.

And then things took a turn for the worse. He was diagnosed with ALS and given two to five years to live. That was over two decades ago!

When he first heard the diagnosis, he had many questions to ask God. *Why did this happen to me? What did I do wrong? All my life I obeyed God's precepts and acted kindly toward my fellow men. So why me?* The illness progressed to the point where, except for his eyes, his body had become totally paralyzed.

One day, his wife, Elisheva, heard her husband straining to breathe. She rushed him to the hospital and had him put on life support. "Why on earth did you resuscitate him?" the attending physician exclaimed. "What quality of life does he have?"

When Rahamim regained consciousness, he was not sure that being kept alive by a respirator was such a good decision. But with time he came to accept his fate with equanimity. "If they had let me die, I would have missed the best and most important years of my life," he is quoted as saying.

Rahamim starts his day praying *Shacharis* (the morning service). His friend Yitzhak comes daily to put *tefillin* (phylacteries) on him, and afterward they learn Torah for an hour.

Then he begins his workday. To date, he has written ten books using gaze-based technology. He answers his extensive emails, and he does artwork on the computer. At 4:00 p.m., family members and friends, children, grandchildren, colleagues, and former students come to visit.

Rahamim is fed through a feeding tube, which takes only three minutes, three times a day. This leaves him time for the things he considers most important. "I want to stay alive for many more years and not miss out on even one moment of my life. Most of all, I want to spread the message of optimism and that life is holy."

Miraculously, Rahamim and his beloved wife Elisheva recently celebrated their sixtieth wedding anniversary. "The message of Judaism," he said, "is that one must struggle until the last breath of life. Until the last moment, one has to live and rejoice and give thanks to the Creator."[8]

SEEING CLEARLY

Helen Keller (1880–1968) was a writer, speaker and advocate for women and for people with disabilities. She was blind and deaf. When Helen was six, Annie Sullivan became her teacher. Helen learned sign language and then Braille, which she mastered in five languages. With Annie's help, Helen was able to graduate from Radcliffe College, part of Harvard University. She wrote several best-selling books and championed the rights of women, the disabled, and minorities. Although public speaking terrified her, she overcame her fears in order to speak out for causes such as the right of women to vote, just working conditions for the poor, and international peace.

Helen could have been miserable, but instead chose to find ways to improve the world. Rather than complain about her lot, she expressed gratitude for her disabilities because they made her who she became. "I thank God for my handicaps," she said, "for through them, I have found myself, my work, and my God."

---

8   Sadly, Rahamim passed away on November 3, 2020, at age eighty-three, having lived with his illness for twenty-six years.

We have a choice. We can choose to blame others or unfavorable circumstances for why our life is not working out, or we can choose to surmount our challenges. If we choose to see ourselves as victims, we will stay miserable, angry, and unable to move forward. If, on the other hand, we choose to view our vicissitudes as opportunities for growth, we will be better equipped to rise above them, and we will be more content and more hopeful.

"I have never believed that my limitations were in any sense punishments or accidents," Helen wrote. "If I had held such a view, I could never have expected the strength to overcome them."

I can think of no one better than Helen Keller to teach us how to really see and how to be truly grateful. I bring here excerpts from an article she wrote, hoping it will inspire you to walk about your day with open eyes and see—become truly aware and fully cognizant of—the beauty to be found everywhere in the magnificent world God created for our enjoyment and benefit. There is beauty all around, but we have to train our eyes to see it. (Some people lament the fact that roses have thorns. Others say, "How wonderful it is that thorns have roses!") We will then spontaneously open our mouths wide and sing new songs of praise and thanksgiving to the Creator.

> *I have often thought it would be a blessing if each human being were stricken blind and deaf for a few days at some time during his early adult life. Darkness would make him more appreciative of sight; silence would teach him the joys of sound…*
>
> *Recently I asked a friend, who had just returned from a long walk in the woods, what she had observed. "Nothing in particular," she replied…*
>
> *How was it possible, I asked myself, to walk for an hour through the woods and see nothing worthy of note? I who cannot see find hundreds of things to interest me through mere touch. I feel the delicate symmetry of a leaf. I pass my hands about the smooth skin of a silver birch, or the rough, shaggy bark of a pine. In spring I touch the branches of trees hopefully in search of a bud, the first sign of awakening Nature after winter's sleep…*

At times my heart cries out with longing to see all these things. If I can get so much pleasure from mere touch, how much more beauty must be revealed by sight...

Oh, the things that I should like to see if I had the power of sight for just three days!...

The first day would be a busy one. I should call to me all my dear friends and look long into their faces, imprinting upon my mind the outward evidences of the beauty that is within them. I should let my eyes rest, too, on the face of a baby, so that I could catch a vision of the eager, innocent beauty...

In the afternoon...I should take a long walk in the woods and intoxicate my eyes on the beauties of the world of Nature...And I should pray for the glory of a colorful sunset.

In the night of that first day of sight, I should not be able to sleep...

The next day...I should arise with the dawn and see the thrilling miracle by which night is transformed into day. I should behold with awe the magnificent panorama of light with which the sun awakens the sleeping earth...

At midnight [of the third day]...permanent night would close in on me again. Naturally in those three short days I should not have seen all I wanted to see. Only when darkness had again descended upon me should I realize how much I had left unseen...

I am, however, sure that if you actually faced that fate your eyes would open to things you had never seen before...Everything you saw would become dear to you. Your eyes would touch and embrace every object that came within your range of vision. Then, at last, you would really see, and a new world of beauty would open itself before you.

I who am blind can give one hint to those who see...Use your eyes as if tomorrow you would be stricken blind...Hear the music of voices, the song of a bird, the mighty strains of an orchestra, as

if you would be stricken deaf tomorrow. Touch each object...as
if tomorrow your tactile sense would fail. Smell the perfume
of flowers, taste with relish each morsel, as if tomorrow you
could never smell and taste again...[g]lory in all the facets of
pleasure and beauty which the world reveals to you...But of all
the senses, I am sure that sight must be the most delightful.[9]

MY STUDENT, MY TEACHER

Years ago, I served as a guidance counselor in a special education unit in a Brooklyn public school. I will always remember one of my students, a girl in fourth grade named Rachel. Short for her age, she was beautiful, with finely chiseled features, intelligent-looking eyes, and an engaging smile. Though she had no learning or behavioral issues, she was mandated for counseling because she had spina bifida. It didn't take long for me to see how much Rachel loved to listen to stories, especially Bible stories, so I bought a book of Bible stories and we spent hours reading and discussing them for the rest of the year.

Due to her illness, Rachel was hospitalized on several occasions and underwent multiple surgeries. Once, when she returned to school after a brief hospitalization, I asked her, "Were you in the room by yourself or was there someone else with you?"

"There was another girl," she said. "She lay with her eyes closed and never spoke. I didn't know if she could speak or hear but I wanted her to have the stories you told me, so I went over to her bed, put my mouth to her ear and started telling her the stories."

Prior to yet another surgery, I noticed she was more anxious than usual and asked her why. "I'm scared," she said. "What if the surgeon gets a heart attack in the middle of the operation?"

I attempted to allay her fears, assuring her that it was highly unlikely and that there'd be a team of doctors who could take over in the unlikely event that it would be necessary. I told her I would pray that all should go smoothly. And indeed, thankfully, everything went well.

---

9   Excerpted from "Three Days to See" by Helen Keller.

Years passed. I was no longer working in the same public school, but I could not forget Rachel. One day, I picked up the phone and called her. She told me she was a student at Kingsborough College.

"Even though it's near my house, I drive there, because it's hard for me to walk. They almost had to amputate my leg. But thank God, in the end, they didn't have to." Then she added, "And now I realize it's all a gift."

"What do you mean?" I asked. "What is the gift?"

"The illness," Rachel said.

"The illness?" I repeated. "What do you mean?"

"It made me *really* appreciate life. I started keeping a special book in which, every day, I write five things for which I am grateful—even if it's only that someone held a door open for me."

At that moment, our roles were reversed: she became my teacher and I the humbled student. Thank you, Rachel. You have taught me an important lesson for life. I shall be ever grateful to you.

THE BEST IN ME

There's a great aphorism of unknown origin that goes something like this: Never ask for a lighter rain, just pray for a better umbrella.

One day, in early spring, I met my friend Tisha, a mother of five children, one of whom is a daughter with Down syndrome. She told me what a challenging winter she had had.

She received a phone call one day from her twenty-two-year-old son, away in college in another state, who was sobbing on the phone. He hadn't cried since he was ten, she told me. He told his mom he didn't know where he was going, who he was, or what he wanted to do, and he had broken up with his girlfriend of four years. At the same time this happened, her twenty-five-year-old daughter suffered a psychotic breakdown and her seventeen-year-old daughter started having seizures. She had eight seizures in one hour and needed to be rushed to the hospital, where they fitted her with a pacemaker.

I said to my friend, "May this be the end of all your suffering. May this be the end of all the difficulties."

Tisha looked at me squarely and said, "No, Sarah, what you are wishing me is not a blessing. It is through difficulties that we grow. I welcome challenges—they bring out the best in me—but preferably not all at the same time!"

FINDING THE GOOD

Rabbi Shimon Schwab became wheelchair-bound in his later years, yet he was always smiling and happy.[10]

His grandson asked him, "How are you always happy? Aren't you upset or angry that you are dependent on others to take you wherever you have to go?"

"I'll answer you with a parable," the rabbi said. "A rich man gave a certain person a million dollars as a gift. After twenty years, he asked the recipient of the gift to give him back ten thousand dollars. Don't you think he was glad to do so?

"God has blessed me with a million dollars. I have eyesight to see the wonders of the world, hearing to enable me to connect to people and to hear lofty thoughts, and to enjoy music and poetry. I have the ability to speak, and to form relationships. I have teeth to enable me to eat, enjoy, and benefit from my food; arms to embrace others; and a brain that makes all this possible. The systems in my body work with clockwork-like precision: the circulatory system bringing blood to the billions of cells in my body, the respiratory system exchanging carbon dioxide for oxygen and enabling me to breathe, the digestive system. God has taken back a little of what He gave me, but I still experience millions of miracles every day. Shouldn't I be grateful? Shouldn't I smile?"

FAREWELL AND THANK YOU

Nov. 5, 1994

My fellow Americans,

I have recently been told that I am one of the millions of Americans who will be afflicted with Alzheimer's disease.

---

10   Rabbi Shimon Schwab (1908–1995) was the *rav* of Kehal Adas Yeshurun, Washington Heights, NY.

Upon learning this news, Nancy and I had to decide whether as private citizens we would keep this a private matter or whether we would make this news known in a public way.

In the past, Nancy suffered from breast cancer and I had cancer surgeries. We found through our open disclosures we were able to raise public awareness. We were happy that as a result many more people underwent testing. They were treated in early stages and able to return to normal, healthy lives.

So now we feel it is important to share it with you. In opening our hearts, we hope this might promote greater awareness of this condition. Perhaps it will encourage a clear understanding of the individuals and families who are affected by it.

At the moment, I feel just fine. I intend to live the remainder of the years God gives me on this earth doing the things I have always done. I will continue to share life's journey with my beloved Nancy and my family. I plan to enjoy the great outdoors and stay in touch with my friends and supporters.

Unfortunately, as Alzheimer's disease progresses, the family often bears a heavy burden. I only wish there was some way I could spare Nancy from this painful experience. When the time comes, I am confident that with your help she will face it with faith and courage.

In closing, let me thank you, the American people, for giving me the great honor of allowing me to serve as your president. When the Lord calls me home, whenever that may be, I will leave with the greatest love for this country of ours and eternal optimism for its future.

I now begin the journey that will lead me into the sunset of my life. I know that for America there will always be a bright dawn ahead.

Thank you, my friends. May God always bless you.

Sincerely,

Ronald Reagan

Nancy Reagan was also eloquent in acknowledging the power of a grateful outlook on life. In a speech she gave to the Alzheimer's Association a year before her husband's death, she expressed her gratitude:

> *Just four months ago, we celebrated our fifty-second wedding anniversary. And as you there understand better than anyone, this was an anniversary that I celebrated alone. Those who have Alzheimer's are on a rocky path that only goes downhill. Ronnie's long journey has taken him to a distant place where I can no longer reach him. We cannot share the wonderful memories of our years together. So many wonderful people over these last ten years have sent Ronnie and me their prayers and best wishes. To those who have been so compassionate, I will be forever grateful for your thoughtfulness. And I want you to take some comfort in knowing that Ronnie is the same gentle, humble, and kind person that he has always been. God has sent us that blessing, for which I am so thankful.*

FREE PARKING

We can cultivate an attitude of gratitude by choosing to appreciate even little pleasures that are part of the human experience.

At a meeting of a mood disorder support group, I struck up a conversation with a wheelchair-bound participant. He shared with me that he is bipolar and developed diabetes from the medication he was prescribed to stabilize his moods. He had been in an accident where he lost both legs and needed to have them reattached. He developed gangrene in one of his legs and subsequently had it amputated.

"Don't you feel you have a rough deal with all these handicaps?" I asked him.

"No," he said. "Everybody is handicapped in some way."

"What do you mean?" I asked.

"Well, we all have our weaknesses. Besides, why shouldn't I be happy? I'm one of the few people who can park anywhere in New York, and I get front-row tickets in the open-air theater in the park!"

WINDOW ON THE WORLD

When my mother was advanced in years, she broke her hip and was hospitalized at Hadassah Ein Kerem hospital in Jerusalem. Whenever I visited her, I would stop to greet Madelaine, the lady who was in the bed on the other side of the partition curtain.

Madelaine hardly ever had visitors. A daughter who was mentally challenged came infrequently and a brother appeared occasionally. Madelaine had spent two years in hospitals, one year in Hadassah Ein Kerem and one year in Hadassah Har HaTzofim. Unable to digest food, she was horrendously emaciated. In addition, she was afflicted with a constant terrible cough.

When I wished her a *refuah sheleimah* (a complete recovery), her response was, "*L'chol am Yisrael v'gam li* (I wish a speedy recovery for all the people of Israel, and also for me)." Ill as she was, uppermost in her mind was the welfare of other people who were sick, and she prayed for their recovery even before praying for her own! If I brought her a glass of water, she was as appreciative as if I had done her the greatest favor imaginable.

The day for her discharge finally arrived. Her brother came to take her home, but it was no easy feat. Since she couldn't walk and there was no elevator in the building in which she lived, her brother had to carry her up to her fourth-floor apartment. Then he had to go down the four flights of stairs again to bring up the wheelchair.

Before she left, I asked Madelaine whether she had a *mirpeset* (balcony). I was hoping she'd be able to sit outside, see the world, breathe in the fresh air, and observe the trees, people walking in the streets, and cars passing by.

"*Ein li mirpeset* (I don't have a balcony)," she said, and added very quickly, "*aval yesh li chalon* (but I have a window)!"

When was the last time we were grateful for a window?

PAINFUL LESSONS: LEARNING FROM ADVERSITY

It's So Easy to Take Things for Granted

In February 2011, on my way to the school where I worked as a guidance counselor, I fell on the ice and broke my hip and my wrist—and that was the end of my hiking days. Prior to my accident, I frequently spent Sundays hiking in Bear Mountain with the Appalachian Mountain Club, which nourished both my body and my soul, and I looked forward to these hikes on a regular monthly basis.

Five years later, in 2016, I was visiting my family in London for Pesach, and when the holiday was over, my family and I went on a mini trip to the Lake District. We spent a whole day out in nature, hiking. I so enjoyed the wooded trails, the spectacular mountainous scenery, shimmering lakes, cascading waterfalls, and fields upon fields of green pastures. We saw many sheep farms and were treated to the sight of newborn lambs standing for the first time on their wobbly feet.

All this, however, came with a price. I developed strong pain in my right upper thigh, which spread to my leg, rendering me incapable of standing up for even one minute without severe pain. Paradoxical as this may seem, I found myself feeling happy because it made me realize what a blessing it was that I had been able to stand up without experiencing pain throughout my life, and I felt such gratitude for this. The pain left after a few days, thank God, and I see it as a gift because it led to my becoming much more grateful for the things I normally take for granted.

The esteemed American psychologist Abraham Maslow pointed out that it is vital that people count their blessings to appreciate what they possess without having to undergo its actual loss. This, I learned, applies to the great blessing of health at least as much as it does to material possessions. I hope I will never take being pain-free for granted again!

Not Alone

Over thirty years ago I had to undergo a dental procedure called an apicoectomy. An infection had formed underneath a tooth that had a root canal and the dentist had to perform surgery on my gums and jaw. Petrified, I kept procrastinating until I could do so no longer because the pain was excruciating. A woman whom I had met at a seminar offered to accompany me to the dentist and accompany me back home. It made such a difference that I wasn't alone. I still feel abundantly grateful to her.

Some Degree of Pain

Once, I woke up with a terrible pain in my neck and rushed to the emergency room in New York University Hospital. I was given an injection of a strong anti-inflammatory, some valium, and a neck brace. It wasn't long before I dozed off. When I opened my eyes, I didn't know where I was.

Thank God, I got home safely. The pain lasted for some time and I was in severe discomfort: the brace was uncomfortable, the pain persistent, and the slightest movement of my head was excruciating. Previously, I hadn't realized just how often we move our heads. Now, in this condition, if I wanted to see something at my side or behind me, I had to turn my whole body around.[11]

In spite of the pain, severe as it was, there was so much for which to be grateful. How fortunate that it hadn't happened right before I was due to travel to London for my nephew Zevi's bar mitzvah. It would have prevented me from traveling. I was also grateful it hadn't happened in London. It would have spoiled my stay, and who knows if in London I would have been given the neck brace, which immobilizes the neck and lessens the pain, making it bearable.

It turned out to be a muscle spasm and not something worse, God forbid, so I have so much to be grateful for. And maybe suffering so much has increased my empathy toward other people in pain.

This episode heightened my awareness of how much I have to be grateful for. The fact that we wake up in the morning without pain—what a blessing! The fact that we can see the sun in the morning, without

---

11 The neck is an interesting part of the body. It connects the head and the heart—the mind and the emotions. From this adverse experience, I connected my mind to my emotions, having learned to be grateful for the ability to move my neck, something I had previously never thought to do.

pain—wow! The fact that we are able to get off the bed without pain, that we are able to dress ourselves without pain, that we can walk, or stand up straight without pain; that we are able to eat breakfast without pain, get to work without pain, go through our day without pain, accomplish what we need to do without pain, and go to sleep at night without pain. How very blessed we are.

There is so much for which to be grateful. Sometimes we need to experience some degree of pain to help us realize how truly fortunate we are.

Even the Bad Is Beautiful

The oldest Holocaust survivor, who died in 2013 at the age of 110, revealed her secret to a happy and long life.

"I look where it is good," said Alice Herz-Sommer, who was born in November 1903, in Bavaria, to a cultured, German-speaking, secular Jewish family. Amazingly, in spite of her two-year incarceration in Theresienstadt concentration camp, and despite the murder of her mother, husband, and friends by the Nazis and the premature death of her son (her only child) years later, she lived a life without bitterness. After surviving the hunger and cold and death all around her, Alice moved to Israel with her son; there she attended the trial of Adolf Eichmann in Jerusalem.

"It is important to us whether we look at the good or the bad. When you are nice to others, they are nice to you. When you give, you receive," she was wont to say. When asked what is the single most important thing in the world, she would answer, "Love. Love, of course."

At age 110, she lived alone in her small apartment in London and was still playing piano two and a half to three hours a day. She considered herself the luckiest person alive.

"When people come to visit," she confided, "people much younger than myself, many like to tell me how bad things are, their many problems, their aches and pains. And I shock them by disagreeing. It's not so terrible. And I'm older than they are. Rather than dwell on problems, why not look for life's gifts? Every day is a present. Beautiful. Everyday life is beautiful. I am full of joy. I am the only one who is laughing; nobody laughs in my building. When we can play music it can't be so terrible.

I love people. I'm interested in the life of other people. I'm always happy, even without music. Music is a dream, it brings us in alignment with peace, beauty, and love. Even when things are very difficult, there are moments. Even the bad is beautiful.

"I am grateful for my mother. I learned from her to be thankful for everything: for seeing the sun, for seeing a smile, a nice walk with someone. Everything is a present, everything. Be thankful for everything. Look for the beauty in life," she advised.

When lying in bed, she exercised her mind by mentally playing pieces of music. Even when very advanced in years, she did not waste her time with thoughts of death or the unknown. "We come from and return to infinity," she believed. "The soul lives on without the body. I come from God and I will return to God. Things are as they are supposed to be. As long as I breathe, I am never too old to wonder, to learn, and, yes, to teach and take interest in others. And music. This is life.

"I see God everywhere; life is beautiful. I know about the bad things, but I look for the good."

A Piece of Bread

If you wanted good farmer cheese you went to Sam's grocery store in Brooklyn; he made the very best. What I liked most about him was that he was always friendly and cheerful, always had a good word for me. No matter how few items I bought, Sam was always nice to me, not like some shopkeepers who are grumpy if you don't spend a certain amount of money in their store. Sam was different. He was kind. Sam knew the value of life, the worth of another human being. I liked Sam.

When Sam retired, I'd often see him standing outside his brother's auction outlet on Sixty-Fifth Street in Brooklyn. His gray hair was thinning, but his brown eyes still sparkled and were as kind as ever. There was an air of serenity about him, as of a man at peace with himself and the world.

Little by little, I pieced Sam's story together. He was a youngster when the war broke out. Separated from father, mother, and sister, he hid in the forests, begging one Polish family after another to take him in, walking barefoot, narrowly escaping death many times. Once, when he was caught and was convinced he was going to be killed, he had a piece of bread in his possession.

"I ate it up," he said to me. "One must enjoy life while one can. After I ate it, I was ready to die."

Sam is not the most learned person, but he has a deep respect for those who do know how to learn, and his faith is strong. "The more I saw," he told me, "the more I experienced, the more I was convinced that there is a God who rules the world. Many a time, ideas that I could never have conceived of by myself came to my mind and saved my life. It was as if somebody put words in my mouth, thoughts in my mind; somebody was there watching over me and controlling my fate.

"Didn't what you've seen and gone through ever make you lose your faith?" I asked him one day.

"No," he said. "My father told me there would come a time when the living would envy the dead and then there would be a war of Gog and Magog and finally Mashiach would come." Sam is certain that Mashiach is on his way and will soon be here.

Sam loves children. He repeatedly told me what a joy it is to see them going to school or coming home with their books. "And even though money is important," he said to me, "there is nothing greater than children, than raising the next generation, ensuring the future of our nation."

A Doorknob on Your Side of the Door

In 1966, Commander Paul Galanti, a twenty-six-year-old graduate of the US Naval Academy, had just completed a bombing mission in Hanoi. Suddenly, his plane was rocked by shuddering vibrations. Paul bailed out of the flaming aircraft and parachuted into hostile territory.

After marching twelve days to Hanoi, he was blindfolded, handcuffed, and incarcerated in a seven-by-seven-foot cell with a concrete slab for a bed. The door, made of heavy, dark wood, had big, rusty bolts and a huge lock. He spent nearly seven years staring at that locked door and others like it.

Twice a day, he was given greasy, watery soup. On occasion, he was treated to stale bread with bits of sand and dirt. Always hungry, Paul shivered through bitter cold winters and sweltered in the scorching summers.

Yet even in the tiny cell he held onto hope. He devised a way to communicate with another American prisoner by means of a code in which the alphabet was transposed into a five-by-five-dot matrix and each letter was represented by tapping on the wall.

One day, he was pulled out of his cell and thrust into an interrogation room. A wooden stool was its only furnishing. The guard shoved him onto it and he sat there for hours with his wrists handcuffed. Each time he drifted into sleep, the guard would beat him on the head with his heavy rifle butt.

Days passed. Paul began to think he might not survive this latest ordeal, but eventually he was pulled off the stool and dragged back to his cell.

In 1973, after 2,432 days of captivity, he returned home to his wife, with whom he went on to have two children.

When Paul got back from North Vietnam, he noticed that Americans seemed to complain endlessly about nearly everything. The motto that had effectively held the POWs together under difficult circumstances—"Unity Over Self"—seemed to have been replaced at home with thinking in the first person singular: me, myself, and I.

Paul and his fellow POWs knew not to take for granted life's simple blessings such as time with family and friends, a warm bed, a hot meal, and, above all, the ability to make choices. "Every day that you've got a doorknob on your side of the door is a day to be thankful," he would say.

Who Packed Your Parachute?

Charles Plumb was a US Navy jet pilot in Vietnam. He flew seventy-five combat missions before his plane was shot down by a surface-to-air missile. Charles ejected successfully, his parachute opened, and he floated down—right into enemy hands. He was captured and spent six years in a North Vietnamese prison. Fortunately, he survived the ordeal and now lectures on lessons learned from that experience.

For years, Charles kept thinking about the man who packed his parachute. More than anything, he wanted the opportunity to show his appreciation and thank him.

One day, Charles and his wife were sitting in a restaurant. A man rose from his seat at an adjacent table, approached Charles and said, "You're Plumb! You flew jet fighters in Vietnam from the aircraft carrier *Kitty Hawk*. You were shot down!"

"How in the world did you know that?" asked Plumb.

"I packed your parachute," the man replied. As Charlie gasped, the man added with a smile, "I see it worked!" To which Plumb said, "It most certainly did. If your parachute hadn't worked, I wouldn't be here today."

That night, Charlie couldn't sleep. "I kept wondering what that man might have looked like in a Navy uniform—a white hat and bell-bottom trousers. I wonder how many times I might have seen him and not even said 'Good morning, how are you?' or anything, because, you see, I was a fighter pilot and he was just a sailor."

Charles thought of the many hours the sailor had spent at a long wooden table in the bowels of the ship, carefully weaving the shrouds and folding the silks of each parachute, each time holding in his hands the fate of someone he didn't know.

Everyone has someone who provides what they need to make it through the day, Charles realized. Now he asks his audiences, "Who's packing your parachute?"

Charles also points out that he needed many kinds of parachutes when his plane was shot down over enemy territory: he needed his physical parachute, his mental parachute, his emotional parachute, and his spiritual parachute. He called on all these supports before reaching safety.

Sometimes, in the daily challenges life gives us, we miss what is really important. We may fail to say hello, please, or thank you; we may fail to congratulate someone on something wonderful that has happened to them; we may fail to give a compliment or just do something nice for no reason.

As we go through this week, this month, this year, let us remember to recognize the people who pack our parachutes.

Gratitude Practices

- Use visual cues. Put a plaque above the hallway mirror with the words GIVE THANKS!
- Put a magnet on your refrigerator door with your favorite gratitude quote, for example, Bill Keane's "Yesterday is history, tomorrow is mystery, today is a gift."

WHAT ARE YOU GRATEFUL FOR?

> I am thankful that my mom was OK when she had sugry for her stomx.
>
> Lucenda, 9

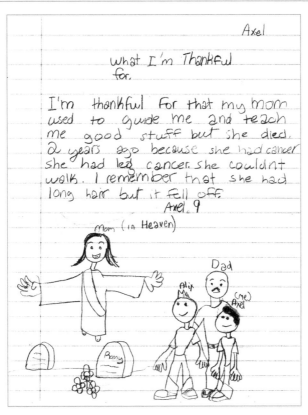

> Axel
>
> What I'm Thankful for.
>
> I'm thankful for that my mom used to guide me and teach me good stuff but she died. 2 years ago because she had cancer she had leg cancer. she couldnt walk. I remember that she had long hair but it fell off.
>
> Axel. 9

"I went to school for web design in Minneapolis, Minnesota. I had to cut my studies short when I was diagnosed with schizophrenia in 2001. I was battling depression at that time. I had symptoms of bipolar disorder and had to get treatment.

I was on Social Security disability. I'm very thankful we have the health-care system we do. And I'm just happy to be here. I didn't think I wanted to be here. I did burning and cutting. I'm thankful I stuck it out, thankful I got the medicine and the treatment I needed."

Norman, 36 years old

"First I thank my parents for bringing me into the world and then I thank Hashem Who created me as a human being.

Not every day is a happy one and we go through difficult things—life one day is happy, one day is sad, and we have problems, like the economy, like sometimes you cannot get your car started, or even big problems like sickness, or a pregnancy that didn't work. I had several miscarriages and my husband was wounded but I thank Hashem we can continue on."

Junior high school teacher

"Even the bad people that come into your life, who give you a hard time. They are there for a reason. There's a lesson in everything; we need to be thankful for everything."

Computer specialist, 46 years old

"I'm grateful that I can serve God; that makes me really happy. When I see people living in the street, I don't like that, I want everybody to be happy."

73-year-old woman

"I'm thankful I can forget that I was abused as a child.

I can't take care of my children, twin boys aged eight years old. They live with their father and stepmother because

I had illness in my mind. I hear voices. They changed my medicine. It's better than the other one."

Hispanic woman on Social Security, 42 years old

"I'm on the street, so that doesn't help me be the kind of father I would like to be, but I'm grateful that my daughter is healthy. I don't get to see her—she's in Arizona and I'm here—but I hear she's healthy."

Homeless man on 14th Street, New York City

"I'm thankful that my daughter was born healthy because I had a high-risk pregnancy. I had a lot of complications and issues. I'm thankful that the delivery was OK and she was born healthy and that I am healthy."

College professor, 35 years old

"I'm thankful for an abundance of simple little things that we take for granted. When I was in the hospital seven years ago for quadruple bypass surgery, the next morning I tried to open the Listerine bottle to wash out my mouth and I couldn't open it. I had to ask the nurse to do it."

Elementary school teacher

CHAPTER 5

Gratitude, Health, and Well-Being

Whenever we are appreciative, we are filled with a sense of well-being and swept up by the feeling of joy.

M. J. Ryan

Among all emotions, there is one which, more than any other, accounts for the presence or absence of stress in human relations: that is the feeling of gratitude.

Hans Selye, author of Stress Without Distress

Gratitude rejoices with her sister joy and is always ready to light a candle and have a party. Gratitude doesn't much like the old cronies of boredom, despair, and taking life for granted.

Rebbe Nachman of Breslov

ONE OF THE MAIN BENEFITS of developing an attitude of gratitude is the positive impact it can have on our mental, emotional, and physical health. King David says countless times in *Tehillim*, "Give thanks to God for **He** is good, for His loving-kindness endures forever." Perhaps this verse can also be interpreted in the following manner: "Thank God, for **it** (thanking Him) is good for us, for our overall mental and physical well-being." There is no need to worry, as we understand that everything is as it should be, and that God is taking care of us.

WHAT MAKES THE SOUL GREAT?

Recent years have seen the emergence of a new school of psychology, referred to as the school of positive psychology. In order to better understand individuals, psychologists have become increasingly aware that we must focus not only on negative aspects of the human psyche but also on the positive.

One construct that has received attention is that of gratitude. Dr. Robert A. Emmons of the University of California, Davis, is the world's leading scientific expert on gratitude. He maintains that gratitude, like other positive emotions such as joy, interest, contentment, and love, appears to have the capacity to transform individuals, organizations, and communities for the better. Gratitude builds and strengthens social bonds in the context of friendships, marriages, and work relationships.

In 2003, he and his colleague, Dr. Michael McCullough of the University of Miami, conducted a series of experiments to see whether a simple practice of gratitude had a positive impact on one's health and well-being: the famous Research Project on Gratitude and Thanksgiving.[1] In their first study, students were randomly assigned to one of three groups:

- One group wrote about five things they were grateful for during the past week.
- One group wrote about five hassles encountered during that day.
- One group wrote about five events that affected them in the last week.

They did this for ten consecutive weeks. Participants in the grateful group expressed more optimism about the future and felt better about

---

1   "Counting Blessings Versus Burdens: An Experimental Investigation of Gratitude and Subjective Well-Being in Daily Life," *Journal of Personality and Social Psychology* 84:2 (2003): 377–389.

their lives as a whole than did students in the other two comparison groups. Furthermore, those in the grateful group spent more time exercising and reported fewer health complaints than the control groups. We see from these studies that a simple weekly intervention showed significant emotional and health benefits.

Emmons and McCullough followed this up with a second study (2003). They increased the gratitude intervention to a daily practice over a two-week period. As in their first study, participants were randomly assigned to one of three groups. The gratitude and hassles groups were the same as in the first study. But in the events group, participants were asked to "think about ways you are better off than others." Feelings that "it could have been worse" often produce a response of gratitude. Participants in the grateful group felt more enthusiasm, were more joyful and energetic, more excited and more determined than those in the hassles condition. In addition, the gratitude group experienced less depression and felt less stressed. This daily intervention showed a stronger effect than the weekly practice of the first study. Those participants who focused on their blessings demonstrated more prosocial behavior. Many reported having helped someone with a personal problem or having offered emotional support to another. Thus, focusing on blessings creates a heightened sense of connectedness to others and strengthens social bonds and friendships. To sum up, inducing a state of gratefulness leads to emotional, physical, or interpersonal benefits.

In light of these studies, the researchers suggest that anyone can increase their sense of well-being and create positive social effects and health benefits just from counting their blessings. They also noted that gratitude encouraged a positive cycle of reciprocal kindness among people, since one act of gratitude encourages another. They suggest keeping a daily gratitude journal in which each night, before going to sleep, you write down at least five things for which you are grateful. People who did this, they found, enjoyed higher levels of physical and emotional well-being.

Other studies show that within a mere few weeks of keeping a daily gratitude journal, people from all walks of life, even chronically ill individuals, report being happier, more optimistic about the future, and more connected to others. Emmons, in his book *Thanks! How the New Science of Gratitude Can Make You Happier*,[2] reported that people who kept a daily gratitude journal had a 20 percent increase in positive mood. "We even saw it [these results] in people with muscular atrophy post-polio syndrome, people who have functional limitations every day and are in pain and fatigued. We had them keep a gratitude journal for twenty-one days and found that this simple intervention resulted in greater amounts of high energy, positive moods, a greater sense of feeling connected to others, and better sleep duration and sleep quality." When we cultivate an attitude of gratitude, we create a slew of positive feelings that are more powerful than positive thoughts, because they generate an overall feeling of well-being.

What is really interesting is Robert Emmons's contention that even pretending to be thankful raises the levels of serotonin and dopamine, chemicals associated with pleasure and contentment. He recommends that we live as if we feel gratitude, and we will end up really feeling it. He even points out that happiness can add years to one's life.

It is not always easy to focus on gratitude, especially when we are dealing with stressful situations such as illness, loss of a job, difficulties raising children, stressful interpersonal relationships, marital strife, etc. However, it is well worth making the effort to work at being more grateful, because, as we have seen, it will make us happier, and it will make us healthier. After all, focusing on the positives in our life stops us from feeling envy, resentment, remorse, or other negative feelings, which are the cause of much unhappiness. Focusing on the benefits we have received from others and from God makes us feel cared for and loved. This positively impacts on our physical and psychological health.

A man once came to his rabbi and said, "Rabbi, I can't take my wife anymore. She is always late when we have to go somewhere. I am so frustrated."

The Rabbi's counsel was simple but wise. "Instead of getting angry at her, bring your attention to all the wonderful things she does for

---

2   Houghton Mifflin Harcourt, 2007.

you. She cooks countless wholesome meals, does your laundry, takes care of the kids, and so much more. You have so much to appreciate, why waste your time and energy on being angry when you could be extremely happy?"

STRESS REDUCTION

According to Emmons and McCullough, gratitude activates serotonin and dopamine neurotransmitters that elevate mood, and gratitude also activates endorphins which make us feel happy and less stressed.

We live with a great deal of stress. Earning a living is stressful, relationships are stressful, raising children is stressful. Stress increases the output of cortisol in our body and too much of this hormone damages our health.

It is well known that illnesses are frequently triggered by stress, so anything we can do to minimize stress should have a positive bearing on our health and well-being. A good way to do this is to cultivate an attitude of gratitude. It promotes better coping with stressful circumstances which, in turn, promotes long-term well-being. Because gratitude may give one a helpful perspective on life, it assists one to repair one's mood following a stressful event, frequently warding off depression.[3] Take a look at the word disease; it can be read as dis-ease—the absence of ease. Disease comes into existence when we are stressed; when we are not at ease.

The deleterious effects of disease are many; they include worry, agitation, and anxiety. Disease can also affect our interpersonal relationships and thereby also affect our health, because having good relationships keeps us healthy emotionally. Stress can take our emotions on a downward spiral and can sometimes lead to depression, and even hopelessness. In extreme cases, it has led to people committing suicide.

Since stress is an inevitable reality in our lives, we need to find ways to reduce it. An effective stress-reduction strategy is to make a concerted

---

3   P. C. Watkins, P. Christianson, J. Lawrence, and A. Whitney, "Are grateful individuals more emotionally intelligent?" (May, 2001), paper presented at the annual convention of the Western Psychological Association, Maui, Hawaii.

effort to become cognizant of the good in our lives and feel grateful for it. According to studies of people impacted by the 9/11 terror attacks, Hurricane Katrina, and Hurricane Sandy, focusing on blessings can help ward off depression and build resilience in times of stress, grief, or disaster.

The number-one killer in the United States is heart attack, frequently brought on by stress. Women, especially those in the work force, report stress as the number-one problem they experience. Working women are juggling careers, managing household chores and child-rearing duties, and many are also taking care of aging parents. This greatly increases their level of stress compared to women of previous generations. The added stress has been linked to a rise in heart attacks in women ever since they entered the work force. A study involving data on 28,732 hospitalizations for heart attack patients aged 35 to 74 between 1995 and 2014 showed an increasing percentage of heart attacks occurring among young women who have entered the work force. These statistics are brought by Melissa Caughey, senior research instructor in the Division of Cardiology at the University of North Carolina, School of Medicine.

As mentioned, we can reduce stress and become healthier by noticing the proverbial silver lining in every cloud, and living in gratitude. When we focus on the good, our stress levels go down and we have a better chance of staying healthy.

To sum up: Clinical trials indicate that the practice of gratitude can have many dramatic and lasting effects on a person's life. It can lower blood pressure, improve immune functioning, facilitate more efficient sleep, lower stress levels, and enhance overall well-being. People who are grateful generally have greater life satisfaction, more optimism about the future, higher self-esteem, and stronger interpersonal relationships. In an article in the *Journal of Clinical Psychology*,[4] Robert Emmons and Robin Stern, associate director, Yale Center for Emotional Intelligence, write that gratitude, more than any other personality

---

4   "Gratitude as a Psychotherapeutic Intervention," 69:8 (August 2013): 846–855.

trait, is strongly linked to mental health. It reduces risk for depression, anxiety, and substance abuse disorders, and it helps people who have these problems heal and find closure. And it can deepen one's trust that goodness exists even in the face of uncertainty or suffering.

Is there a link between gratitude and the well-being of people who find themselves undergoing extremely difficult life challenges, for example, those who take care of patients suffering from Alzheimer's disease? Jo Ann Tsang of Baylor University studied the effect of gratitude on caregivers—specifically those who cared for Alzheimer's patients. Tsang found that writing about gratitude was sufficient to have an impact on caregivers' health.

Grateful people often feel the desire to give—even a physical part of themselves. Eleven years ago, one of the teachers in a yeshiva where I worked, Mrs. Leah Grossberg, the mother of six children, donated a kidney to save the life of a total stranger. When I asked her what prompted her to do this, she said, "If I am in good health, how can I not thank Hashem for my good health? That's my way of thanking Hashem."

Here is something amazing about the power of gratitude to improve one's health: "The more gratitude the recipient of an organ transplant feels toward the donor, the quicker will be his or her recovery." Seventy-four recipients of an organ, either a heart, lung, liver, kidney, or pancreas, who expressed gratitude directly or even indirectly by keeping a gratitude journal, reported feeling physically better and functioned at a higher level than those who did not.[5]

A study in 1995 by Dr. Rollin McCraty of the Institute of HeartMath in Boulder Creek, California, showed that just five minutes of gratitude can have a calming effect on our neurological and endocrine systems. Being in an appreciative state creates whole body resonance where our heart, breathing, blood pressure, and brain rhythms are synchronized, as is the case when we are deeply relaxed or sleeping. On the other hand, when we are feeling stressful emotions such as frustration, resentment, anger, guilt, or anxiety, heart rhythms become more erratic.

---

5   Stephen Post and Jill Neimark, *Why Good Things Happen to Good People* (Broadway Books, 2007), p. 30.

In another fascinating study, focusing on appreciation for just fifteen minutes resulted in increasing levels of an immune antibody called secretory IgA, which is one of the body's primary defenses against invading microbes. After practicing appreciation for fifteen minutes a day for a month, thirty individuals had a 100 percent increase in a beneficial hormone called dehydroepiandrosterone (DHEA), as well as a 30 percent reduction in the stress hormone cortisol.

The psychologist Russell Kolts of Eastern Washington University studied individuals who suffered from post-traumatic stress disorder. He found that those who scored high on gratitude had significantly lower symptoms of the disorder. Similarly, a study of Vietnam veterans with PTSD showed that to the extent to which they experienced gratitude they had better daily functioning. And A. M. Masingale[6] studied PTSD in student survivors of trauma and found that grateful individuals had significantly lower PTSD symptoms than less grateful individuals. These studies give credence to our premise that gratitude plays a role in alleviating (some of the) distress caused by PTSD. Yet another study showed that a practice of gratitude improved the body image of people who had bulimia.

GRATITUDE AND DEPRESSION

Nearly one in twelve US adults reports suffering from depression. Major depressive disorder affects 17.3 million adults or about 17.1 percent of the US population age eighteen or older in a given year.[7] Depression accounts for close to twelve billion dollars in lost workdays each year.[8]

Practicing gratitude may decrease the likelihood of depression because it provides more focus on and enjoyment of benefits received, and directs one's attention away from lack. Being content with their lot in life, grateful people generally do not make comparisons with

---

6   A. M. Masingale, R. L. Kolts, and P. Watkins, "Gratitude and post-traumatic symptomatology in a college sample" (December, 2001). Paper submitted for presentation at the convention of the International Society for Traumatic Stress Studies, New Orleans.

7   National Institute of Mental Health, "Major Depression" (2017).

8   *The Wall Street Journal* (2001), National Institute of Mental Health (1999).

others who have more—unlike ungrateful people. The danger of making comparisons is that it leads to feelings of deprivation, frustration, anger, guilt, and depression. Practicing gratitude, on the other hand, can sometimes ward off depression by directing one's attention away from one's problems, instead focusing on the good they are receiving from others. Grateful people tend to have satisfying social interactions with others because they are not preoccupied with themselves. These relationships contribute to feelings of overall long-term well-being.

It is important to note that people who feel fortunate and grateful for their lot in life and for all the good they experience—not excluding difficulties and challenges, which they view as opportunities for personal growth—are going to feel joyful and happy, and this has a major bearing on their long-term health. As we have seen, happiness is curative. People who are happy tend to be cheerful and upbeat and their optimism makes them feel strong emotionally and physically; it imbues them with confidence and hope.

In a survey of American teens and adults, over 90 percent of respondents indicated that expressing gratitude helped them to feel "extremely happy" or "somewhat happy,"[9] and people who are happy heal faster when illness strikes.

A remarkable example of this is Norman Cousins, journalist and author of many books. If you want to know more about the healing power of happiness, read his best-selling book, *Anatomy of an Illness as Perceived by the Patient: Reflections on Healing and Regeneration*. In 1964, following a very stressful trip to Russia, he was diagnosed with ankylosing spondylitis, a degenerative disease causing the breakdown of collagen, which left him immobile and in constant pain. The doctors gave him only months to live. But he believed otherwise. Aware that happiness has a major role to play in the healing process, he left the hospital, with his doctor's consent, and checked himself into a motel opposite the hospital. He spent his days watching humorous films that lifted his spirits and made him laugh a lot, and he defied the doctor's

---

9   G. H. Gallup (1998).

negative predictions. His condition steadily improved and he slowly regained the use of his limbs. Within six months he was back on his feet, and within two years he was able to return to his full-time job at the *Saturday Review*. Despite the dire prognosis that his illness was rapidly disintegrating the connective tissue of his spine, Cousins regained the full function of his body. He lived twenty-six more years, ultimately dying from a heart attack in 1990.

His story baffled the scientific community and inspired a number of research projects. In a radio program broadcast in August 1983 in Los Angeles, California, Cousins claimed that ten minutes of belly laughter gave him two hours of pain-free sleep when nothing else, even morphine, could help him. This is a striking example of the impact of a happy disposition on the healing process.

We now know that one's psychological state has a bearing on one's physical state. As we have seen, grateful people (because they focus on the positive) are happy people, and happy people heal faster. So, if you want to be healthier (and who doesn't?) use the practices and imagery exercises in this book to cultivate an attitude of gratitude and reap a multitude of rewards. Make the effort, give yourself the time. You are worth it. Resolve to let no day go by without you saying thank you to somebody. It may be the only thank you this person has heard in a long time.

Gratitude Practices

- Tell a friend how you felt about an experience you shared with this friend that led you to be grateful. By expressing gratitude to your friend, you are giving them a gift.
- Sing a nursery rhyme and see what feelings about your childhood it conjures up.
- Sing and dance for a few minutes each day. It doesn't have to be for a long time; two or three minutes is also good. But do it each day.

CHAPTER 6

How to Develop an Attitude of Gratitude

When a person doesn't have gratitude,
something is missing in his or her humanity.
A person can almost be defined by his or her
attitude toward gratitude.

Elie Wiesel

PEOPLE GENERALLY don't give much thought to gratitude, perhaps because they like to be seen as self-sufficient. Nobody really likes the feeling of being beholden to anyone. In addition, the Western culture in which we live celebrates consumption and makes us feel that whatever we have is not enough. Having more is seen as better, but we can never have enough. Finally, we tend to see ourselves as the entitled owners of things rather than the recipients of gifts.

It's easy to have non-grateful thoughts. Sometimes we think we deserve better circumstances; sometimes we're disappointed because things have not turned out the way we wanted. But the truth is, compared to all the people alive today in the world, Americans are among the richest one percent. Besides, people cannot have so little that they have *nothing* at all to be grateful for. Even the poorest Americans have better nutrition, more freedom, better medical care, and better housing than the middle classes of Third World countries.

HINDRANCES TO GRATITUDE

Certain character traits make it difficult for some people to feel and express gratitude. With self-understanding and effort, and the will to change, these characteristics can be ameliorated, allowing a person to experience a happier and more thankful existence.

The Narcissist

Narcissists, egoists, and young children all believe that the world revolves around them. With maturity, most children realize that there are other people whose feelings and needs have to be considered. Adults who experience narcissistic tendencies must recognize this character deficiency and come to terms with the idea that they are *not* the center of the universe.

It might be useful to find a partner with whom to study a *mussar sefer* (book of ethics) such as Rabbi Moshe Chaim Luzzatto's *Mesillas Yesharim* (Path of the Righteous) or *Ahavas Chessed* (Loving Kindness) by the Chafetz Chaim.

The "Entitled"

A good way to correct feelings of entitlement is to realize that everything is given to us by God not because we deserve it, but as a gracious gift, given to us gratuitously. Another way is to view anything people do for us or give us as a gift, conferred upon us out of the goodness of their heart, and not something that's coming to us by right.

Whether it's time, money, respect, or love, we should give back a thousandfold to those who give to us. When receiving a kindness, reciprocate by doing a kindness, so as not to let any favor go unrecognized or unreciprocated.

The "Victim"

Too many people go through life blaming others for their misfortunes:

- "My life is a mess because my father wasn't home enough when I was a child."
- "I'm a failure because my teacher said I'd never amount to much."

- "I'm full of anger because my parents got divorced when I was four years old."
- "I don't have confidence because my father was an alcoholic."

The list goes on and on. With a mindset like this, we're never going to be grateful.

The best way to let go of feelings of victimization is to realize that we ourselves are the orchestrators, the producers, and the actors of our lives. Success and happiness lie within us. External conditions are the accidents of life, its outer trappings. Resolve to keep happy, and your joy will form an invincible host against difficulty.

Character cannot be developed in ease and quiet. Only through experience of trial and suffering can the soul be strengthened, ambition inspired, and success achieved. Once we understand this, we might even be grateful for our challenges.

The Envious

Instead of enjoying the blessings God showers upon us each day and appreciating the gift of life itself, envious people are the instruments of their own misery. Such people have an *ayin ra*, a "bad eye," as mentioned in *Pirkei Avos* (Ethics of Our Fathers).[1] They torment themselves by always looking at what others (neighbors, family members, colleagues) have and convince themselves that they must have the same things in order to feel happy. But in truth, to be happy, we need to enjoy what we already have. People who always want more rob themselves of their own happiness.

Jealousy and envy are two different things. Envy is coveting what another person has; jealousy is not wanting the other person to have it. The following parable that appears in *Orchos Tzaddikim* (The Ways of the Righteous), the classic sixteenth-century book of Jewish ethics, illustrates this idea:

> *An envious man and a jealous man appeared before the king. The king said to them, "One of you may make a request, which*

---

1   2:14.

I will grant—provided that I give twice as much of the same to your companion." The jealous man did not want to ask first, because he didn't want his companion to receive twice as much. The envious man did not want to ask first, because he wanted for himself what belonged to both of them. Finally, the envious man pressed the jealous man to make a request. The jealous man asked the king to pluck out one of his eyes, because then his companion would have both eyes plucked out.

A strange story, indeed, but one that illustrates how low one can fall when begrudging the good another person has.

We need to be careful not to transgress the Biblical commandment against coveting what our neighbor possesses. Toward this end, it may be helpful to adopt the words of our forefather Yaakov—"*Yesh li kol*" (I have everything)[2]—as an affirmation. Write this phrase repeatedly twenty, thirty, forty times or more, and say it over and over again. Do this as a ritual every morning for three weeks (perhaps in front of a mirror), and allow yourself to really feel it. It will help you not to be envious, and you will become more grateful and more appreciative of who you are and what you own.

The Overly Independent/Arrogant

Individuals who have had to fight for their independence may feel there is something wrong with them if they cannot do everything by themselves. Rabbi Eliyahu Dessler and Rabbi Shlomo Wolbe explain that when a person does you a favor, it may feel tantamount to saying that you couldn't do it on your own; you needed someone else to help. It's a blow to the ego.

It takes humility to say thank you. An arrogant person is often an ungrateful person. It would benefit such individuals to realize that we are interdependent social beings engaged in an ongoing dance of give and take. Life is not only about getting. It's about giving, receiving, and repaying.

---

2 *Bereishis* 33:11.

Arrogant people like to take all the credit for their achievements themselves, and fail to show gratitude to people who helped them along the way, or to God. President Lincoln, in his 1863 inaugural Thanksgiving Day proclamation, warned against this vice:

> *We have been the recipients of the choicest bounties of heaven; we have been preserved these many years in peace and prosperity; we have grown in numbers, wealth, and power as no other nation has ever grown. But we have forgotten God. We have forgotten the gracious hand which preserved us in peace and multiplied and enriched and strengthened us, and we have vainly imagined in the deceitfulness of our hearts, that all these blessings were produced by some superior wisdom and virtue of our own. Intoxicated with unbroken success, we have become too self-sufficient to feel the necessity of redeeming and preserving grace, too proud to pray to the God that made us.*

Here is a story told by the Chassidic teacher Rabbi Refoel of Barshad[3] that depicts the perils of thinking too highly of oneself:

> *When I get to Heaven, they'll ask me, "Why didn't you learn more Torah?" I will tell them I was not bright enough. Then they'll ask me, "Why didn't you do more kind deeds for others?" I will tell them I was physically weak. Then they'll ask me, "Why didn't you give more charity?" And I'll tell them I didn't have enough money for that. And then they'll ask me, "If you were so stupid, weak, and poor, why were you so arrogant?" And for that I won't have an answer.[4]*

---

3   Prominent Torah scholar, famous for his saintly conduct, who lived in Europe in the nineteenth century.

4   Alan Morinis, *Everyday Holiness: The Jewish Spiritual Path of Mussar* (Boston: Shambhala, 2008), p. 48.

The Non-Forgivers and Judgers

People who cannot forgive themselves or others become mired in a bog of recrimination and finger-pointing. Unable to see the good in themselves or their peers, they tend to be unaccepting of their own failures as well as the shortcomings of those around them. They are so busy judging, they lose sight of the beauty inherent in themselves and in every one of God's creatures. One way to overcome this is by remembering that we are created in the image of God, as is all of mankind. This should give them a feeling of how lofty and important they are.

Bearing a grudge stops us from feeling gratitude. Whatever "they" did is over. Holding on to the past stops us from living the present. Forgiving is a decision, it's a choice, it helps us move on with life in a healthy and positive way.

It's important not to define our life by how we've been hurt. The danger, if we fail to do this, is that we assume the role of victim and give away our power to the offending person. But if we forgive, we will reap the rewards of emotional freedom and spiritual healing. We might even find compassion and understanding. We must not focus on the person who wronged us but on the lesson we can learn from this person or event.

MAKING THE EFFORT TO FORGIVE

Refusing to forgive allows the person who was hurtful to continue to hurt us. If we remain unforgiving, we might bring anger and bitterness to other relationships, thereby forfeiting enriching connectedness with others. Our life might be so wrapped up in the wrong that we can't enjoy the present. One of the ways to get over the upset is to ask ourselves, "How will I feel in six months' time, in one year, in three years, in ten?" No one ever gets to the end of their life and thinks, "I wish I stayed angry longer."

The Talmud points out that "one who overcomes his natural tendencies [in this case, the tendency to hold on to a grudge; and instead of begrudging, forgives], all his sins are forgiven."[5]

Forgiving can be extremely difficult when having been hurt, but it is possible that people who have developed an attitude of gratitude will be

---

5   *Rosh Hashanah* 17a.

more able to forgive than those who have not developed such an attitude. When we realize that holding on to our pain hurts us more than it hurts the person who has wronged us, we may more readily forgive the person for what he or she has done.

Action Steps to Forgiveness

1. Acknowledge the hurt.
2. Don't minimize or deny the wrong that was done against you.
3. Don't make excuses for the offender.
4. Write it down. Journaling is a great way to work through anger and hurt. Sometimes writing a letter (usually not to be sent) to the offender is helpful; it helps work through your thoughts and feelings.
5. Identify your emotions. When someone does something to hurt you, you might experience anger. This is not wrong; it is a normal response to the offense.
6. Cancel the debt. Write a "blank check" of forgiveness. List the offenses they have done and then write, "Canceled."

The Self-Deprecating

Individuals with low self-esteem are unaccepting of themselves, frequently focusing on their failures and not on their strengths. They may feel they are not worthy of being the recipients of gifts, kindnesses, or even compliments.

Besides learning to appreciate the good things in our environment and in our lives, we need to learn to appreciate ourselves for being the wonderful human beings that we are. This self-appreciation should not be dependent on our achievements. Rather, it should come from a commitment to look for and appreciate the greatness in ourselves, not only the greatness in others. We are created in God's image; there is a Godly part in all of us. As Rabbeinu Yonah writes in *Shaarei Teshuvah* (Gates of Repentance): "The first gate is that people should know their own value, their high level and their greatness and importance and how beloved they are to their Creator."

Appreciating ourselves comes with practice. One of the best ways to achieve this is to learn how to accept compliments gratefully, gracefully, and graciously. Trust and believe the person giving you the compliment. Silence the inner critic. If you silence the critical voice inside you, you'll be able to hear the kind words being spoken. If somebody compliments you on something you're wearing, for example, refrain from downplaying their words by disagreeing or minimizing them. Don't say, "It's really old," "It didn't cost much," "Do you really like it?" or "It's a hand-me-down." Say, "Thank you"—and nothing else.

Accepting a compliment graciously is not the same as looking for approval from others. That doesn't work because it can never be enough. Self-esteem needs to come from within ourselves. If we don't accept ourselves, we waste a lot of energy trying to prove that we are good enough. But we will never be happy like this. To compensate for low self-esteem, we might go around tooting our own horn, and people mistakenly may get the impression that we are arrogant.

CASE STUDY

In my capacity as a guidance counselor, I worked with an eight-year-old girl who had a number of academic, behavioral, and social issues. She was always neatly attired, with a colorful bow in her hair that matched her outfit, and when I told her how lovely she looked, she rebuffed me, saying, "That's not me; that's my mother." When I complimented her on the wisdom of something she told me, her response was, "That's not me; someone told me." When I said something positive, she commented, "That's a compliment," and when I asked her to elaborate, she said, "People give compliments to make someone feel good."

I told her that while this may be true for some people some of the time, I really mean what I say all of the time. I didn't compliment her merely to make her feel good, I explained. I said it because it's the truth, and if it made her feel good, so much the better! I emphasized that my words are sincere; I only make positive remarks when I feel the truth of what I am saying.

Not long after this, a miracle happened. When, a couple of weeks later, I said something positive to her, she surprised me by replying,

"Thank you." I was ecstatic. She was beginning to recognize and accept her own value. What a profound difference this was making in her current life! Within weeks her classroom behavior improved dramatically. She didn't throw desks anymore, didn't make noises, stopped being disruptive. She sat quietly in her seat and attempted to complete her work. She smiled more often. The feelings of frustration were transformed into feelings of self-acceptance. She showed signs of being a happier child all around.

Such a change in self-esteem would increase her ability to be in a nurturing relationship going forward, because in order to be in a healthy relationship, it is necessary to have feelings of self-worth: "I am a worthwhile human being, I deserve to be treated well and with respect and be listened to. I have a contribution to make. What I say and feel is important. I am worthy of receiving gifts and being appreciated."

Rebbe Nachman of Breslov points out that to be happy and joyful, one needs to see the good in all people, including oneself.

"And the way to sing the song of joy is by seeking the good in all people, especially in ourselves. Each good point is one note in the song of life."[6]

Author's Thanksgiving Prayer

Today is a new day, a priceless gift from God.

Today I will love myself. I am precious in the eyes of God, so how can I not be precious in my own eyes?

Today I will choose how I want to feel, what I want to do, what I want to let go of.

Today I will commune with God. I will put myself in His Hands. I will not be afraid.

Today I will not let any human being, no matter who they are, upset me or hurt my feelings or make me feel bad. I will sow seeds of generosity, compassion, and kindness, and make somebody's heart sing.

Today I will act with courage and faith, stay focused on my project, and move forward on the path I have chosen.

---

6   *Likutei Moharan*, part 1, lesson 282.

IMAGERY EXERCISES TO INCREASE SELF-ESTEEM AND FEELINGS OF SELF WORTH

Having feelings of self-worth is essential if one is to feel hope, optimism, and joy. Developing self-worth will also make you feel gratitude for being the wonderful person that you are. As you start to believe in yourself and become more confident, you may find yourself becoming more creative. You will find that as you learn to love yourself, you will be better able to love other people, and your relationships will become richer and more satisfying.

Do these exercises and feel more alive, more energized, and more grateful. You will become a much happier person for it.

Induction (to be done before every exercise): Close your eyes. Breathe out slowly through your mouth three times, and:

- See yourself looking for and finding the spark of goodness in yourself and in everyone you know. Even include people you find it difficult to relate to.
- See yourself growing gracefully, creatively, and joyously into your authentic self, awakening to your unique giftedness and inner beauty.

See three things for which you appreciate yourself. Know that if you appreciate yourself, you will be better able to appreciate others.

- Imagine you're making a list of things someone or some people could do for you that would elicit feelings of gratitude in your heart.
  - See yourself doing three of these things for other people.
  - See clearly what you're doing and to whom.
  - Resolve to do these things concretely in your life.
  - Imagine you are writing down the action you're doing, the name of the person to whom you're doing the action, and where and when you are doing it.
- Recognize and acknowledge your character strengths.
  - See how the three "Cs"—confidence, courage, commitment—are helping you succeed.

- See, sense, and know that God resides in you if you make space to let Him in.

CHANGING NEGATIVE BEHAVIORS

It's hard to feel grateful at the same time that one feels frustrated, resentful, angry, or guilty. We need to clean out these negative emotions to make space for more positive ones, such as joy and gratitude.

Several steps are necessary in order to let go of the negative behaviors and mindsets that prevent us from feeling gratitude. Asking God to help us—and thanking Him in advance for His help—is always a good idea. Work on *kavanah*. This Hebrew word means intention, direction, and will. Make sure your will to develop an attitude of gratitude is strong. Nobody gets very far with a weak will!

Anytime you wish to achieve a particular goal do the following exercise, preferably with closed eyes.

Imagine you are in a large green meadow
choose a tree you like and walk over to it
with a piece of white chalk draw a circle on the trunk
this is your target.

Now take five steps back
remove your bow and arrow from your quiver
while keeping sight of your target
engrave your goal on the arrow.

Make sure your arrow, your eye, and the target are in a straight line.
When you see the line becoming a point, release the arrow.
If your eye, the arrow, and the center of the target
are in a straight line, becoming a point,
you reach your goal.

The first step is to become aware of the behavior that needs changing. Second, we have to really want to change. But at the same time, we must understand that change is incremental; it doesn't happen overnight. We may improve for a while and then slip up. Knowing that this is normal should help us not to despair or give up trying. We don't want to castigate ourselves for not being perfect and we need to not be hard on ourselves.

We have to be confident that change is possible. We become more confident by reminding ourselves of the times we worked on ourselves and succeeded, and by remembering our accomplishments in any area of endeavor. If we slip (and we will, at times, because we're only human), we should not feel guilty, because guilt can paralyze us and keep us stuck. We want to recognize what happened, correct it, move on with our lives, and be grateful for the ability to change, to move forward and to grow.

It's good to give ourselves credit when we succeed. For example, every time we could have acted in a judgmental manner but didn't, we should pat ourselves on the back for exercising self-discipline and self-control.

IMAGERY EXERCISES TO CLEAN OUT NEGATIVE EMOTIONS

Do the following imagery exercise with the intention to cleanse yourself of negative emotions and free yourself up to feel gratitude and love. You will be doing yourself a great service. I recommend that you do this exercise three times a day—morning, noon, and night—for three weeks. Then take a break and let the images work by themselves in the subconscious mind, before doing another cycle of three weeks.

Induction (to be done before every exercise): Close your eyes. Breathe out slowly through your mouth three times, and:

1. See yourself going back in time, five years at a time, starting from now and going back until you reach age five.
2. See the people, the places, and the situations where you experienced frustration, resentment, anger, or guilt.
3. Now, take a broom and sweep these emotions away, or clean them out with a shower of sunlight or clear, clean rainwater. If they are deeply ingrained, you may wish to use a strong detergent.
4. See and sense how this is cleansing you inside and out.
5. Breathe out and see yourself growing up quickly from age five, moving forward five years at a time until you reach today.
6. You have cleaned up each situation where you felt frustration, resentment, anger, and guilt. See what is replacing the frustration and resentment, the anger, and the guilt.

NATURE OR NURTURE?

I read about a person who, when asked whether the glass was half empty or half full, responded by saying, "I'm thankful I have a glass!"

Is gratitude something you're born with or is it acquired? In M. Scott Peck's book, *In Search of Stones*, the author speculates that some people carry a gene for gratitude that others lack. Perhaps that partially explains why some people who have very little in terms of material comfort, or have gone through major health or other challenges, are able to appreciate life, and others who seem to be blessed with everything go through life angry and resentful.

Even if some people are born naturally more optimistic, more positive, and more thankful, the good news is that we can all learn how to become more grateful. Some of us may have to work harder than others. Whatever we're least good at, that's what we need to practice most. Robert A. Emmons, author of several books on the topic of gratitude, admits that gratitude is not something that comes naturally to him. He has to keep working at it, he says.

Why are people not grateful? One reason is that we do not take time to reflect on our blessings. We are so busy making a living, so preoccupied with amassing material things (many of which we don't actually need), that we fail to reflect on what's really important in our lives. Lacking the quiet time necessary for reflection, we live in a state of non-awareness.

When our minds are busy, strange things happen. Some of us have had the experience of searching for our glasses only to find that we are wearing them. I even had the experience of looking for the phone and discovering that I was holding it in my hand. Have you ever gone into a room to get something, only to find you've forgotten what you came in for? These things happen because our minds are constantly flooded with thoughts.

There are a number of things we can do to rouse ourselves.

Become Aware of Our Lack of Awareness

Human beings need to be taught to be grateful. We tend to take for granted things we get on a regular basis. We get used to things quickly.

If you live next to the train tracks, with time you'll stop hearing the train. If you stick your hand in a bowl of hot water, after a couple of minutes you will not feel the heat. If you smell the intoxicating scent of a rose in full bloom, no matter how long you keep your nose stuck in the flower, your olfactory sense will eventually cease to register the scent. Desensitization, built into human beings, deadens our awareness over time. Without awareness, there can be no joy and no gratitude.

Wake up and open your eyes! It's not difficult to find things for which to be grateful. We just have to pay attention and notice what's around us. Think about the incredible gifts that civilization gives us. The lights are on—we have light simply by flipping a switch! The shower's hot—we turn a faucet and have hot water, cold water, drinkable water; we don't have to go to the well to bring it to our homes! Millions in the world will never experience this. How can we adequately express thanks for the ample availability and incredible variety of food? And for our taste buds, which enable us to enjoy it?

Look at the sky. Notice how it is different from moment to moment, with clouds coming and going. This formation of clouds in the sky will never be the same as it is right now. Look at the clouds, and marvel at the water cycle. Rain, evaporation, condensation, cloud formation, rain...

PRAY

Praying is one way we can connect to our deeper selves and develop a feeling of gratitude and thankfulness. Starting our day by thanking God for the gift of life makes us consider what we have to be thankful for: our health, the air we breathe, the fact that we were able to get out of bed unassisted. How thankful we need to be when we have clothing to keep us warm and a roof over our heads; the ability to talk, see, hear, taste, and a sense of smell; friends and family, teachers; the ability to enjoy the beauty in nature, a sunrise, a sunset, a starlit sky, music, poetry, books...the list is endless.

PRACTICE MINDFULNESS

Mindfulness is a wonderful way to enhance our feelings of gratitude. Anyone can learn the practice of mindfulness.

Simply sit comfortably in your chair, close your eyes, and pay attention to the natural rhythm of your breathing, your in-breath and your out-breath. If a thought comes, acknowledge it and bring your attention back to your breathing. Some people find it helpful to focus on their nose or stomach. As you become aware of the rhythm of your breathing, your in-breath and your out-breath, notice how your mind becomes calmer and you feel more at peace.

A few minutes a day suffices to achieve major benefits.

Since I've been practicing mindfulness:

- I enjoy whatever it is that I'm doing more of the time because I'm more present in the moment.
- I enjoy my food more. I eat more slowly and enjoy the different tastes and textures. When I *bentch*, I don't merely thank God for the food. I thank Him for *every* morsel of the food, because I've enjoyed every morsel.
- My relationships have improved because in my interactions with people, I'm thinking about them and not about me. Mindfulness has helped me become a better listener. I listen in order to understand and I'm able to connect more deeply to whomever I'm listening to.

Perhaps you are saying, "I don't have the luxury of time to be mindful." But that's exactly when you need to practice mindfulness! Five minutes daily is all you need, and if that is too much, three minutes a day would also be beneficial—as long as you practice regularly each day. Those few minutes will bring you untold benefits. You will go about your day feeling calmer, happier, more creative, more present—and more grateful!

KEEP A GRATITUDE JOURNAL

I started keeping a gratitude journal many years ago, hoping it would assist me to live in gratitude consciousness more of the time and make me a more grateful person. I began with just one or two journal entries daily and wrote whatever things I was grateful for that spontaneously entered my mind. I just had to start, and it was amazing what followed;

ideas, thoughts, sensations, feelings, and emotions entered my consciousness like a gushing waterfall.

I encourage you to start a daily gratitude journal and reap its many rewards. Each day—try to make it the same time each day—write down five things for which you are grateful. These can be little or big—the sun was shining when you woke up, the coffee tasted good, a meal you enjoyed, a meaningful conversation with a friend or colleague, the joy of completing a project at work, noticing the many ways God takes care of you as you go through your day. If you do this regularly, you will naturally repeat yourself. This is perfectly okay. The important thing is that you keep the emotions fresh. Try to elaborate and be as specific as you can. Where possible, include your feelings.

Some people stick to lists; others write paragraphs, compose poetry, or write descriptive essays. The important thing is to keep writing and to keep being grateful.

CULTIVATE A "GOOD EYE"

A good eye (*ayin tovah*) is the ability to find the good in every person and in every situation. In a relationship that is less than perfect, try to find one positive personality trait, one situation where the person acted kindly to you or to someone else. Let this be at the forefront of your thinking and focus on it as much as possible. If a negative thought intrudes, recognize it for what it is, and return to the positive feeling. When we do this, we ourselves will benefit, because although we cannot change the other person, we can change ourselves, and by doing so, the other changes, too.

Colette's Way

My mentor Colette lived in Jerusalem. Students from all over the world flocked to study with her. And some came to be healed. In the twenty-four years I was privileged to know her, I never heard her say anything derogatory about any of her students, acquaintances, or family members—or anyone. One day I asked, "How come, in the many years I've known you, I've never heard you make even one disparaging remark—ever?" Colette was an expert in the science of morphology;

she accurately read faces and was well aware of our flaws and foibles. In answer to my question, she said, "I see at first the good."

Her focus was on the good, on our inherent strengths, never losing sight of the heights to which we could aspire. By relating to our potential, she was able to bring out the best in her students. If like her, we train ourselves to see at first the good—sooner or later we will find the good.

It's so easy to neglect being grateful to those nearest and dearest to us, because we tend to have a lot of expectations of them, some of which can be fulfilled and some of which cannot. We may feel let down or betrayed when these expectations are not met. When this happens, it is good to realize that they did the best they could with the wisdom they had at that particular time—just as we do the best we can with the wisdom we have at any particular time.

Let's say you have a sibling with whom you don't get along. As long as you focus on his or her negative character traits and the negative aspects of the relationship, you will never bridge the gap and the relationship will never improve. But if you're able to find one good quality in that person's make-up and you direct your attention to it and focus on it, you can achieve a closer relationship.

"He Is Like You"

A friend of mine told me about her disappointment in her brother for never being there for her, and about her resultant anger toward him. I pointed out that when she travels to London to visit her family, she takes her anger with her. Her brother picks up on her negative energy, and becomes even more indifferent, so she ends up never having her needs met. But it is in her power to change things, I told her.

"Before you board the plane," I advised, "take time to focus on your brother's good qualities. Then, when you visit him in London, he will pick up on your positive energy. This will likely lead him to engage in positive conversation with you and not be so aloof and indifferent. He may even invite you to stay over at his place."

And this is exactly what happened!

Why? Because when we feel a certain way about someone, we put out certain vibes, which the other person is able to pick up. If we harbor anger in our heart, even if we don't openly display it, the object of our anger will sense it and, in turn, feel angry at us. The reverse, of course, is also true. If we feel warmth in our heart toward someone, even if we haven't expressed any warm sentiments, the person will feel it.

We are enjoined in the Torah to "love your neighbor as yourself." This can be interpreted as "love your neighbor—*he is like you*"—with good points and foibles. Focus on the foibles and you have an unsatisfactory relationship; focus on the positives and you will surprise yourself by what a positive relationship you can create.

I once read about twin sisters in their nineties. They hadn't spoken to each other in sixty years. Now that they were ninety-three, they finally decided to break the silence. Sixty years wasted, bereft of warmth and friendship!

BE SATISFIED WITH WHAT YOU HAVE

In *Pirkei Avos* 4:1, our rabbis pose the question: "Who is happy?" The response they give is that the truly happy person is someone who is not only content with what he has but actually rejoices in it.

It's human nature to always want more. Our Sages put it like this: "He who has a hundred wants two hundred, and he who has two hundred wants four hundred."[7] They didn't say, "If you have ten you want twenty." A hundred is ten times ten; it's a lot, but it's human nature not to be happy with what we have, even if it's a lot.

The Greek philosopher Epicurus said, "Do not spoil what you have by desiring what you have not." The consumeristic society in which we live gives us the message that we must have more and more things; that we cannot be satisfied with what we have. Madison Avenue bombards us with the notion that our happiness is contingent on owning the newest gadgets and the latest-model cars, leading many of us to live above our means. We purchase things with credit cards even though we don't have the money to repay them, and then worry about how

---

7   *Midrash Koheles Rabbah* 3:1.

we're going to extricate ourselves from the financial morass of our own creation. We work longer and longer hours because we desire more and more money to buy more and more goods, many of which we don't really need.

This way of living puts an inordinate amount of stress on the family. We become demanding, frustrated, and short-tempered when we don't have something we crave. We become guilt ridden when we can't give our spouses and children everything they want. We feel inadequate, and find we are in a low mood, even depressed, much of the time.

Happiness comes from wanting what we have and not from having what we want. Looking over one's shoulder to see what the next person possesses, keeping up with the Cohens, is the cause of much unhappiness. We need to adjust our gaze, to focus on the good stuff, putting our attention on the things we have and not on the things we don't have. Developing an attitude of gratitude will increase our enjoyment of the good, our enjoyment of others, of God, and of our very lives.

Our mindset should be one where we recognize that God gives each one of us exactly what we need to be able to fulfill our unique purpose on this earth. If God didn't give it to us it means we don't need it. With this attitude, no one will be envious because we'll realize that we don't need what someone else has.

SMILE!

We have the power not only to make ourselves happy but also to gladden others simply by smiling. It's contagious.

Our Sages understood this well. They have taught us to greet every person we encounter with a pleasant, cheerful face: "*Hevei mekabel es kol ha'adam b'sever panim yafos.*"[8] And they even go further and say to greet every person with joy: "*Hevei mekabel es kol ha'adam b'simchah.*"[9]

As a young child, I came across the following short poem by J. Graham Simpson:

---

8   *Pirkei Avos* 1:15.
9   Ibid., 3:12.

Smile awhile!

And while you Smile—

Another Smiles;

And soon there's Miles

And Miles of Smiles,

And Life's worth while

Because you Smile.

I have discovered that when I smile, my mood instantly improves. Smiling is an easy and sure way to make myself feel happy, and the effects are seen immediately. Although this may appear simplistic, it really isn't. When I awake in the morning and recite the *Modeh Ani* prayer with a smile, it makes me feel joyful. And when I say it without a smile, it does not have the same effect. I've shared this with some of my friends and suggested they might do the same—and they have told me how smiling when saying their prayers engenders feelings of gratitude and happiness in them. So I start my day smiling and feeling grateful, blessed, and cared for by the Almighty. I'm ready to face the challenges of the day.

A smile costs nothing, but gives much.
It enriches those who receive,
without making poorer those who give.
It takes but a moment,
but the memory of it sometimes lasts forever.
None is so rich or mighty that he can get along without it,
and none is so poor but that he can be made rich by it.
A smile creates happiness in the home,
fosters good will in business,
and is the countersign of friendship.
It brings rest to the weary,
cheer to the discouraged,
sunshine to the sad,
and is nature's best antidote for trouble.
Yet it cannot be bought, begged, borrowed, or stolen,

for it is something that is of no value to anyone
until it is given away.
Some people are too tired to give you a smile.
Give them one of yours,
as none needs a smile so much as he who has no more to give.

Author Unknown

GAIN A HISTORICAL PERSPECTIVE

One way to develop feelings of gratitude is to study Jewish history.

Think about the past, see the hand of God, recognize the Divine Providence, perceive how, since time immemorial, God has saved us from all our enemies, from physical and spiritual destruction. We must open our eyes to see the countless miracles He has performed on a national level, and continues to perform to ensure the continuation of our people. We are witnessing the fulfillment of God's promise that He will never forsake us. Our hearts should sing with exultation and gratitude. We see that God is not only the Creator of the world; He is also the God of history.[10]

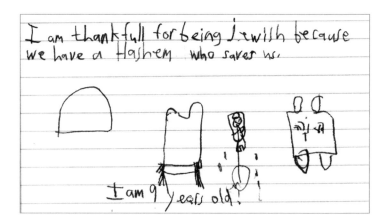

I am thankfull for being Jewish because we have a Hashem who saves us.

I am 9 years old!

---

10   Furthermore, studying science, physics, chemistry, biology, mathematics, music, astronomy, geography, and history will open our eyes to get a glimpse of the magnitude of the greatness of God and enhance our feelings of gratitude to Him.

Miracle in Meah Shearim

On February 8, 2001, a car bomb packed with a whopping 15 kg of explosives exploded in Jerusalem in a narrow street in the densely populated religious neighborhood of Meah Shearim. According to eyewitnesses, debris from the explosion soared 150 meters into the air. Miraculously, no one was killed, and only one person was slightly injured.

The local residents, mindful of their near-brush with disaster, broke forth in spontaneous singing, dancing, and praises of God which went on for two hours. The next day, signs were posted on trees and telephone poles, enjoining people to recite *Tehillim* 21, which talks about God's kindness in saving His people from the onslaught of their enemies who rise up against them to destroy them, and concludes with, "We will sing praise to God on account of his mighty deeds."

LETTERS OF GRATITUDE

John Kralik, a lawyer who lived in Los Angeles, thought he had nothing to be thankful for. He had hit rock-bottom. He was miserably overweight, totally broke, and going through his second divorce. He lived in a dismal apartment with no air-conditioning. He couldn't afford to pay his employees bonuses because his clients were not paying their bills on time—or not paying at all.

How did he turn his life around?

He found the answer in developing a gratitude practice. He decided that next year he would make it his goal to write one thank-you note each day, for a total of 365 thank-you notes for the year. He wanted to find a reason to be thankful for every single day. He said that writing thank-you notes over the course of the year taught him to appreciate the good things in life.

Kralik remarks that our natural tendency is to notice the seven, eight, or even nine bad things that happen to us each day. But we can change. We can choose to focus on one good thing to start off with, and then go on from there to two good things or three good things or maybe even more, each and every day.

Letters of appreciation do not have to be pages long. A short letter of even two or three sentences can make the person who did you a favor feel appreciated, if it comes from the heart. The main thing is it should be sincere.

Don't do it as a chore—make it fun! Challenge yourself to write thank-you notes for thirty days.

The following are suggestions of what you might say:

I haven't acknowledged you sufficiently for…*[Select whatever is appropriate]* listening to me when I needed someone to listen to me / your words of encouragement when I needed them most / forgiving me when I was remiss / the confidence you instilled in me by believing in me / loving me through thick and thin / introducing me to a wonderful person (or wonderful people) / your nonjudgmental acceptance of me / respecting my wishes and respecting me as a person / your empathy / your generosity / your trust and your loyalty / showing me how to lighten up / being happy at my good fortune / the fun times we shared together…

Read John Kralik's book.[11] It will inspire you as it did me.

SAMPLE LETTERS

A letter I received after giving a presentation at a city-wide conference of educators:

> *This was by far the most user-friendly workshop I have ever taken. What you talked about, and the magnificent way you presented the material and developed the concepts, was so important, so practical, and so meaningful. I can't wait to get back to the classroom and to my students to start to implement your novel ideas. You have inspired me, and all of us, with your creativity, positivity, and passion for teaching. We hope you come back on a future occasion.*

---

11   John Kralik, *365 Thank Yous: The Year a Simple Act of Daily Gratitude Changed My Life* (Hachette Books: New York, 2010).

A letter I wrote to my mother's home attendant:

> *Dear Darlene,*
>
> *Thank you for your love, for your patience, for your beautiful smile, for being so dedicated, so loyal, and so caring. We will always appreciate the wonderful way you took care of our mother. God bless you.*

The following is a letter written by Karl Barth, the great Protestant theologian of the last century.

> *My dear Mozart,*
>
> *What I thank you for is simply this: whenever I listen to you, I am transported to the threshold of a world which, in sunlight and storm, by day and by night, is a good or ordered world. Then as a human being of the 20th century, I always find myself blessed with courage (not arrogance), with purity, with peace. With an open ear to your musical dialectic, one can be young and become old, can work and rest, be content and sad: in short, one can live.*

MONITOR YOUR WORDS

We have to be very careful with the words we speak about ourselves and about others. It's so easy to fall prey to gossip because it's all around us. We need to be on the lookout and refrain from listening to or speaking gossip.

We have the power to create our world with the words we speak. To be people who speak positively, who respect those around us and live a life of true gratitude and appreciation, we need to refrain from engaging in gossip. People who gossip revel in negativity. Negativity doesn't lead to gratitude.

PAY IT FORWARD

> Thankfulness may consist merely of words. Gratitude is shown in acts.
>
> *Henri Frederic Amiel*

> Kindness is the golden chain by which societies are held together.
>
> *Goethe*

Giving of your time and energy to help others stems from appreciating the abundance we have been blessed with, which generates the desire to give back.

The law of behavioral reciprocity dictates that people should help those who have helped them. If you can't, then help somebody else. It may not be possible to return a favor done for you by a stranger—for example, you're waiting for the bus and by accident you drop your bag of fruits and vegetables and a stranger helps you pick them up. Obviously, you can't return that favor; but, by way of gratitude, wouldn't it be nice if, during your day, you looked for someone to whom you could be of assistance?

As William Penn explained: "I expect to pass through this world but once. If, therefore, there can be any kindness I can show, or any good thing I can do to any fellow being, let me do it now, and not defer or neglect it, as I shall not pass this way again."

Do a random act of kindness to someone you know or even to someone you don't know. Let someone go ahead of you when you're standing on line at the store or at the post office. Pay somebody's bus fare. Buy a homeless person breakfast, lunch, or dinner. When you order a cup of coffee, pay for the person behind you.

My ninety-year old aunt, an avid reader, told me that she had gone to the Brooklyn Public Library at Grand Army Plaza. When she came out of the building, she realized she didn't have money for the bus fare to return home. She is a shy person by nature, but feeling she had no choice, she reluctantly approached a teenager walking in the street and told him her predicament, asking if he'd be so kind as to give her money for her carfare, and he willingly obliged.

"I can't thank you enough," my aunt said, to which the teen replied, "The best way to thank me is by doing a kind deed for someone else."

Were we to do a kind deed for someone we know, or even someone we don't know, on a regular basis, we'd be making the world a better place. And we ourselves would be the beneficiaries because performing acts of kindness would make us happy. There's nothing as heartwarming as the knowledge that we did a kind deed for someone. Helping others—whether it's by acknowledging them or by doing them a favor (even a very small favor!), by listening to them, by giving words of encouragement or support, by recognizing their good qualities and letting them know it—makes *us* feel good that we made *them* feel good.

Gratitude Practices

- Before getting out of bed in the morning, look around your room and focus on the things in your room that make you happy. Carry this feeling with you throughout the day.
- Get into the habit of taking two or three minutes a day to reflect on what you love about your life. You may want to do this three times a day: in the morning before getting up, at noon before eating lunch, and at bedtime. This simple practice can change your attitude, and by changing your attitude you can change your life.
- Should you be in a negative frame of mind, focus for a moment or two on three things you're grateful for. Shift your attention to the positives in your life.
- Make it a daily ritual to spend two or three minutes focusing on all the wonderful things and people that surround you.
- Write your own book of positivity, in which you list things you appreciate in everyone you know, even people you don't like. Find something positive, something you do like—and if you can't, make it up. Once you start, it will become easier.

IMAGERY EXERCISES TO HELP YOU CULTIVATE
AN ATTITUDE OF GRATITUDE

Here are some exercises to help you put your knowledge of the importance of gratitude into practice. The exercises have been grouped into topics, namely: cultivating an attitude of gratitude, the importance of living in the present, gratitude to those nearest and dearest, how gratitude enhances all relationships. The more often you do the exercises, the more you will be cultivating an attitude of gratitude and the more gratitude you will feel in your heart. This will make you the kind of person other people want to be around, and you yourself will become happier and more cheerful. Do one or two exercises a day. You may take a month to do them all.

Induction (to be done before every exercise): Close your eyes. Breathe out slowly through your mouth three times, and proceed.

Cultivating an Attitude of Gratitude

- Imagine you are an artist painting a picture of gratitude, then paint your picture concretely.
- Imagine you are a sculptor creating a three-dimensional manifestation of your gratitude. Describe what you have created.
- See how developing tolerance, patience, and acceptance of yourself and others enhances your relationships and makes you a more grateful person.
- See how you create harmony and happiness in your world by cultivating an attitude of gratitude.
- See yourself beginning each day with a smile, happy and grateful for the gift of a new day, the gift of new opportunities, and, yes, the gift of new challenges. See how you are using these opportunities and challenges for your personal spiritual growth.
- Visualize three things for which you are most grateful about your life, about yourself, about your spouse, about your friend, about your child.
- Imagine you are designing a package of thank-you cards. Describe the artwork and the messages you are writing on each one.
- Hear yourself asking: "To whom am I grateful? For what am I grateful? Who has helped me that I didn't thank enough?"
- Imagine a world devoid of gratitude. How would it look? Breathe out. Now visualize a world where all of mankind feels and expresses gratitude. How would this look?
- Imagine you are sitting with someone with whom you are close. Hear yourself asking: "What have I received from this person? What have I given this person? What, if any, trouble have

I caused her or him? What happiness have I given them?" Are you discovering you owe this person more than you thought? If yes, repair it now.

The Importance of Living in the Present

- Sense and know how living in the past robs you of the gift of the present. See, sense, and know how worrying about the future is the thief of the now.
- See and know how living in the now gives rise to gratitude and is the only way to really live. See yourself fully living this moment. What are you doing? How are you doing it? How do you feel?
- See and sense how living with frustration, resentment, anger, and guilt depletes you of your energy and cuts you off from your creativity.
- Imagine you are weeding your spiritual garden. See what you are doing to uproot frustration, resentment, anger, and guilt, making space for love, hope, joy, and creativity.
- See how, when you fail to exhibit gratitude, you've lost an opportunity to rectify Adam's sin of ingratitude.
- See your accomplishments in front of you. Identify each one and see the people that have helped you on your path. Offer a silent prayer of thanks to each one.
- See the fortuitous circumstances that have enabled you to reach some of your goals. Feel how fortunate you are to have been at the right place at the right time.
- See yourself spreading your warmth and light and love into your immediate surroundings and into the world. See how, when doing this, you attract healing and serenity back to yourself. Sense the contentment, inner peace, and harmony that this is creating, and feel blessed now and forever more.

Appreciating Family and Friends

- See, sense, and know how, by appreciating your spouse, you bring harmony into your home. See the different ways you are appreciating your spouse, your parent, your child, your friend, yourself.

- When was the last time you did your spouse a favor? What was the favor? Why did you do it? What was the effect?
- When was the last time you did a favor for a parent? What was the favor? Describe the effect.
- Identify a favor a family member did for you. What was the favor? What was the effect it had on you? How did you express your appreciation?
- Identify positive character traits, talents, and giftedness you received from your parents, grandparents, great-grandparents, and all your ancestors going back to your very roots—and be grateful. Find a way to express your gratitude to your parents for passing on the good genes you have been blessed with.
- See your teachers in front of you, starting from your kindergarten teacher through high school. Find a way to thank each one for what they have given you. Be specific.

Gratitude Improves Your Relationships with Friends and Acquaintances

- See and sense how, when you appreciate others, you not only make them feel happy, but you yourself become happier. See how your appreciation enriches your relationships.
- Identify some of the more meaningful ways you've been there for others at a time of need. How does this make you feel?
- Identify some of the kind things others have done for you. Breathe out. Go over to each one and thank them in a meaningful manner.
- See how something you thought was a small favor actually meant a great deal to the recipient of the favor. See how each time you perform even a small favor, you create goodwill, peace, and harmony.
- Imagine you are in a theater on stage behind the curtain. As the curtains rise, you see the theater is packed with people whose

lives you've touched. Hear them, one by one, tell you how much you've meant to them and why.

- Imagine you are on a stage behind the curtains in a large auditorium or theater. The curtains rise and you see the place is packed with people from whom you've benefited in either a small or big way. Imagine you're writing the names of these people in a beautiful cloth-bound notebook. Hear yourself telling each person what they've done for you and how you appreciate this.

- See yourself making a mental list of your friends. Imagine you are writing next to each name what it is you like about him or her. Now, find a way to express your appreciation to each one. Make sure you express your appreciation in the manner specifically suitable for each person.

- See yourself going back in your life five years at a time, starting from now and going back to your birth. At each stage, identify a person or people from whom you have benefited. See the person, the situation, the place. Tell each one what they did, why it was important to you, and thank them in the way you know best.

Seven Principles for Cultivating Gratitude[12]

1. Gratitude is independent of our objective life circumstances.
2. Gratitude is a function of attention.
3. Entitlement precludes gratitude.
4. We often take for granted that which we receive on a regular basis.
5. Gratitude can be cultivated through sincere self-reflection.
6. Expressing gratitude through words and deeds enhances our experience of gratitude.
7. Our deepest sense of gratitude comes from an awareness that we have not earned nor do we deserve all that we have been given. Our blessings are bestowed upon us as a freely given gift from God.

---

12   From the ToDo Institute.

CHAPTER 7

Raising Grateful Children

Let's be grateful to those who give us happiness; they are the charming gardeners who make our soul bloom.

Marcel Proust

Of all the crimes that human creatures are capable of committing, the most horrid and unnatural is ingratitude, especially when it is committed against parents.

David Hume

JUST AS WE NEED to teach our children cooperation, kindness, respect, honesty, and manners, so too, we need to teach them gratitude. It is part of being a mensch. In our consumerist society, this is easier said than done. Madison Avenue's message that we cannot be happy with what we have creates dissatisfaction and unhappiness because happiness is not about having what we want—it is about wanting what we have.

Many parents give their children everything they desire—except what children crave the most, which is time spent together. Children get used to acquiring the latest gadgets, the newest technological game. As soon as a new item comes out, they must have it, or else they're miserable. Many of these amusements run into the hundreds of dollars. So why do parents buy them for their children? Could it be to alleviate their guilty feelings for not spending more time with them? Or perhaps they think they are bad parents if they don't give their children everything they want, everything their neighbors' children have. Is it in order to assuage their own insecurity and convince themselves that they are good parents that they give in to their children's demands?

An effective tool in teaching our children gratitude is to say no from time to time. My parents taught my siblings and me to appreciate what we had by not giving us everything we desired. We had to work and save up money to get things we wanted. Two of my siblings delivered newspapers before going to school. One of my sisters served tea at the London Zoo to save up money to buy a phonograph. When I wanted to go to Paris upon graduating high school, my father said, "If you have money, you can go." But I didn't have the money. Undeterred, I did some research and found out about a children's camp in Paris and applied to be a counselor. That's how I got to realize my dream: by working for it.

The danger of giving our children everything they crave is that they'll develop a sense of entitlement and never be satisfied with what they have. Many years ago, I asked one of my fourth-grade students to help straighten out the classroom. When he finished putting the desks in neat rows, he turned to me and asked, "What are you going to give me?" It made me wonder, how are we raising our children if they can't help without expecting something in return? I offered him some cookies, but he wanted something more, something bigger, something better. Perhaps he even wanted me to give him money.

MODELING GRATEFUL BEHAVIOR

How can we teach our children to appreciate what they already have? Lecturing rarely works. The most effective way is for us to become good role models, to demonstrate that we are grateful for what we have and for who we are.[1] It's not enough to tell them to say thank you. Children

---

1   Rabbi Samson Raphael Hirsch says that the most important thing a person has to learn is to stand on two feet. How do children learn to walk? Not because we instruct them. They watch

need to see the adults in their life expressing gratitude to their parents, siblings, friends, neighbors, and colleagues, as well as to people who provide services, such as the storekeeper, the mailman, the garbage collector, the bus driver, the cleaning lady, and the babysitter. Children need to see us never take anyone for granted. Gratitude needs to lead to an action, a kind word, a thank-you card, a phone call expressing appreciation, a little gift.

Toddlers and very young children may not be able to understand the concept of gratitude, but as they get older it is something they can comprehend. Parents and teachers should emphasize, by word and example, the importance of showing appreciation wherever it is called for.

When your spouse does something considerate, express your appreciation and let the children see this and learn from you. When children see their mothers and fathers expressing thanks to each other for the things they do around the house—such as taking out the garbage, cooking dinner, setting the table, washing the dishes, doing the laundry, stocking the pantry, mowing the lawn, running errands, carpooling, and helping the children with their homework—they will hopefully learn by osmosis not to take anyone for granted.

Gratitude is required for good even when it's mixed with some bad. We put this into practice by giving partial credit. For example, if your spouse did you a favor but it wasn't one hundred percent perfect, a thank you is still in order. Too often, spouses take for granted daily "small" favors that they do for each other. Each expects the other party to do the chores and errands they usually do because "it is her or his job."

My father related to us, as we were growing up, that when he was a child neither he nor his siblings were allowed to leave the table before thanking their mother for the food she cooked for them and for her hard work in the kitchen. Out of consideration and gratitude to our mother, our father never started to eat before she was seated at the table. He always started the Seder by thanking our mother for her hard work getting the house ready for Pesach.

---

how we're doing it, and they imitate us. That's how children learn. Whether it's to walk or whether it's to show appreciation, they learn by us modeling for them.

Teach children through example by acknowledging the good they do. When your child does a household chore, even if it's one of his or her assigned tasks, say thank you. Thank your child for helping with younger siblings and for helping around the house. For example:

- "I really like the way you showed patience and didn't get angry."
- "You did a great job setting the table."
- "You're such a big help to me when you take care of the baby."

The list is endless. The important thing is to be specific.

PRACTICAL TIPS FOR TEACHING CHILDREN GRATITUDE

For children even as young as four years old, a simple way to lay the groundwork for gratitude is to ask them what their favorite thing was about the day and what they are looking forward to tomorrow.

My niece and nephew in London have five children ranging in age from fourteen to two. Every week at the Shabbos table they have a ritual whereby each child in turn thanks each one of their siblings for a specific kindness they received from them during the week.

Encourage your children to give a gift back to a classmate who has given them one. In this way you train them to be caring, giving, and generous, and in so doing you also teach them not to take anyone for granted. You might even want to give them an extra snack to give to a classmate who doesn't have one.

Teach children to admire the wonders of nature: the blue sky, fluffy silver clouds, nimbus and thin wispy cirrus clouds, and white puffy cumulus clouds that look like cotton wool. Point out colorful flowers, varieties of trees, the ever-so-green grass and shrubs, and the many birds we find in the outdoors. Where possible, take your children to the park, to the zoo, to the aquarium, and to museums to open up their eyes to the magnificence of the world around us.

Buy each of your children a nice book to use as a gratitude journal and encourage them to be as specific as possible when recording what they are grateful for. Listing "my friends, my mother, my school, my dog" can lead to gratitude fatigue. Focusing on the details, such as, "My dog licked my face when I was sad," or "Princess jumped up and wagged her tail when I came home from school," or "My dad took time off from work to buy my new game," helps children to delve deeper, keeps their writing fresher, and keeps them enthusiastic about writing in their gratitude journals.

Make a bulletin board for things your children are grateful for. Have your children draw pictures or cut out magazine pictures of things they appreciate and let them pin them on the bulletin board. You can also put pictures of people you love on your bulletin board. Place the bulletin board in an easily visible spot. Periodically set aside time to admire the objects and pictures together with your child.

When putting your child to bed at night, spend a few minutes telling him or her about good things that happened to you during your day and encourage your child to do the same. An example of this might be finding a colorful leaf in the street on the way to school, noticing a bird's nest or a spider's web, or even finding a ladybug.

Have children get into the habit of writing thank-you notes. Try to make it a fun activity. Encourage them to specifically mention the gift and say something appreciative about it, because this makes the note so much more meaningful. Writing thank-you letters to babysitters, teachers, relatives, tutors, neighbors, and other caring adults helps children appreciate all the people who care about them.

FROM A TEACHER'S PERSPECTIVE

If you are a teacher, be thankful you have students. Be grateful for their health and their willingness and their lives. Be grateful for the opportunity to interact with these young people in a positive way. Once you've stated the thought, "I am grateful for each and every one of my students," treat them like you are grateful. Show them courtesy, provide as much personalized attention as you can, and go the extra mile to give them incentives to make them want to be in your class.

I'm Thankful For...

In the course of my work with children in elementary and junior high schools, I often ask them what they're grateful for and I share a few of the things that I appreciate to give them some ideas. Frequently, the response they give is "I'm thankful for my family and friends," and indeed this is something we should not take for granted. However, I try to get them to dig deeper. Here are some of their responses:

> "I'm thankful that I'm the oldest because I feel like a mother and get to boss my siblings around. I like to boss them because it's fun."
>
> *Deborah, age 9*

> "For sad, because you have to have feelings."
>
> *Deena, age 13*

> "That I'm allowed to hold my baby brother."
>
> *Naomi, age 7*

> "That God woke me up this morning."
>
> *Daniel, age 8*

> "I'm thankful that I can pray to Hashem."
>
> *Moriah, age 6*

> "I'm thankful that you said thank you to me because I held the door open for you."
>
> *Sharona, age 5*

"I'm thankful that I'm nine so I could stay for the whole wedding when my aunt got married. Only nine and up can stay for the whole wedding."

Ruth, age 9

"I'm thankful that I can hear my mother say 'I love you.'"

Alex, age 12

"I'm thankful that my sister got married because now she's nicer to me because she can't show she's mean in front of her husband."

Brenda, age 10

"I'm thankful for my brain."[2]

Kaylee, age 4

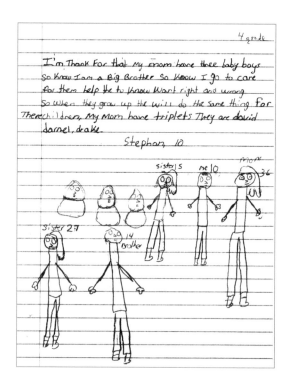

---

2   When I asked her why, she said, "Because I like it, and for my neck because that's where I eat."

I am thankfle for being alive and being able to sing and dance and do Gmynasticks.

Sarala, 11

I am thank full for a baby
And a birth day and that I am a
girl and that I goto school and
I have friends and a family and
I am not pore. and a mother and father.
And therapist who help me And that I am
me and everything I have!

Devora, 9

I am gratful for my family
They are annoying avry day. my mom
warts me to do the dishes. But its
my brother's turn.
Blake, 9

I am thanckfell that my
parins Love me thay hug me
and kiss me

Sarala, 8

I am thankfull for
SoterDay and Sunday

Yonthan, 7

Yonthan   Dean

I am thankful for my mom and my frog and my hetghog

Daniel, 8

Mom   frog   hetghog

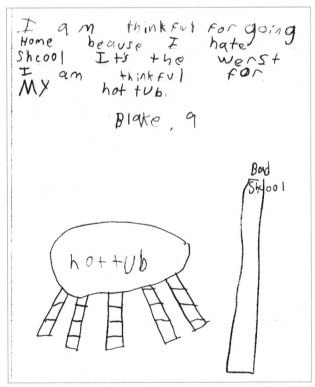

I am thinkful for going Home beause I hate Shcool It's the werst I am thinkful for MY hot tub.

Blake, 9

hot tub

Bad Shcool

I am thankful for: My family and
that I Like roller costers
and I am helthy and I have
energy and my close. and I
Lean Istuff in School.

Rebecca, 9

I am, thancfall that
I have 6 Grand prents
Joey, 6

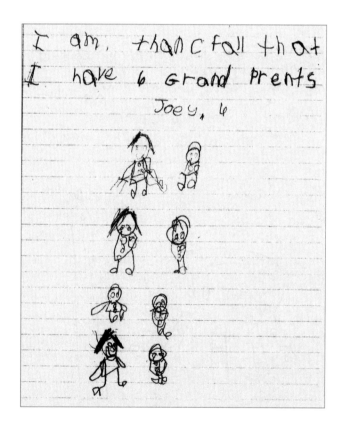

I'm thankful for a can comunicate with other people I'm not def I can understand I have a brain I'm not stupid. I can play piano I'm A A great student. My body works I have great grandmothers and Great Grand Fathers. I'm Thankful I can Walk. I'm Able to teach my self. I'm proud that I learned how Do speak spanish. I'm able to go on grips.

Deana age 8

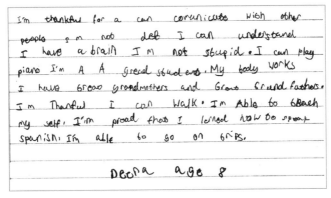

I am thankful also for my playground. I am thankful for my mom.

Daniel, 8 yers old

* I am thankful for all parts of my body.

* I am thankful for having a great grandmother.

* I am thankful for having a coat or else I will freeze.

* I am thankful for going to school so I can learn not like other people in some countries where children have to go to work.

Name: Bathsheva
Age: 14

I'm thankful for my brother he comes for a little while helps me with my homework he plays with me. I'm thankful because I have a wonderful family. I'm thankful for my coach in soccer. I'm thankful because he is in boarding school, and he's safe. (My Brother) Lemuel, Age 9

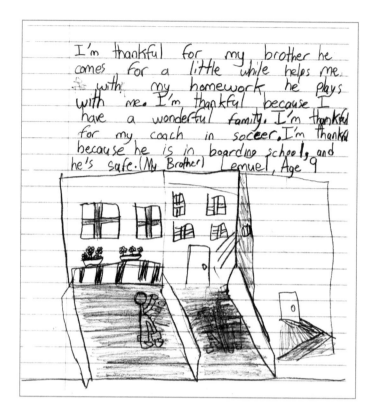

I'm thankful for
Toys
Rivkys dog
School so most over
Vickashen
askape from day camp
Perl!, 8

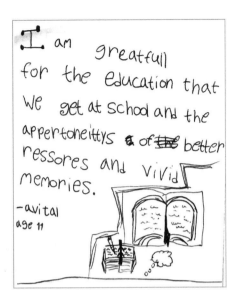

I am greatfull for the education that we get at school and the appertoneittys of the better ressores and vivid memories.

—avital
age 11

I am thankful for my pet kitten and my nintendo.

Aerial, 8

I am thankful that I can keep my desk clean
I am thankful that I have prety lihin

chany, 9

I'm thankful that I have the energy to play flute.

I'm thankful for my great grandmother and great grand father.

I'm thankful that I have a good taste in fashtion.

Chavi, 9

I am thankful for my two dogs that I love alot.

I am thankful for the food that my great grandma gives me.
I am thankful for the toys I get from my family.

Lexi, 10 years

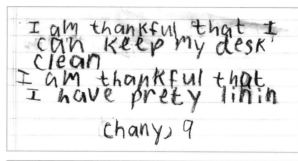

I em thankful for a lot
of things like if sum Bude
He lps me.

Leor, 7 yers oue

EXPRESSIONS OF GRATITUDE

Children I am privileged to work with have chosen many different ways to express gratitude to me and to others. Some verbalize their appreciation. A nine-year-old girl was moving and going to a new school. Her parting words to me were, "I think you are the angel God sent for all the children on the Earth." Some choose to draw a picture; some write me a letter; a ten-year-old girl invited me to her birthday party. Another drew a picture and wrote me a letter, saying: "You are my fairy godmother. Anybody who is not like you, should change and become just like you." An eight-year-old boy bought me a fuchsia-and-orange-colored coleus plant for Mother's Day. I kept this plant until it withered, and I kept the little black plastic holder until the soil fell out. It brought back memories of the special relationship I had with this sad little boy whose parents were going through a nasty divorce. I used to take him to the teachers' room and make tea for him with just the right amount of sugar (four heaping teaspoons is how he liked it). And then one day he said, "I just can't be sad when I'm with you."

A seven-year-old girl I counsel went on a cruise to Russia and Finland with her family during the summer vacation and brought me back a pen with a little doll at the top. She said, "I got you this because you gave me a butterfly so I wanted to give you something, too."

I had the opportunity to talk about gratitude to the fourth graders of a school where I work as a counselor. Sometime later, a young girl from this class sought me out to tell me that her family had spent Shavuos in a hotel. "I remembered what you taught us about gratitude," she said, "so I went over to the cleaning lady and said, 'Thank you for keeping the hotel so clean.' And the cleaning lady had tears in her eyes and said, 'You're the only person who ever said thank you to me!'"

Here is a sampling of letters of gratitude I received from children I've worked with over the course of several years. I cite them in order to demonstrate the capacity of children to express gratitude, and to highlight the unique way each child chooses to do so. Notice how these children are able to get in touch with deep feelings and sentiments, which they express with honesty and sincerity—no phoniness here. Their letters demonstrate an ability to connect with others, even to adults.

From: Samantha   Age 9.
                How I feel about
Miss Berkwits.

Miss Berkwits the nice teacher.
If she was to come to my
to my house, I would,
put a welcome mat in front
of my Bed room, make up
the bed and Spray air frensher
for her. I will make shure
She is comfortable. I will also,
make Shure she sleeps well.
I will take care of her for as
long as she stays. O and she is
always welcome to stay Because
She treats me nice so that
will be my chance of Being
nice to her.
                Jo : Miss
                Berkwits

    The End.

angela Hodges

class 107 grade 9 th

JS 4?

4/12/89

My counselor is real nice.
when I have a problems she
listens and then tries to
give me the answers that
will best help me. when
ever I don't tell her she
won't force me. she is a real
nice person to have when you
need help! what is this
lades name, Ms. Berkovits.

angela

fiftteen   years   of   age

Ms. Berkovits

You have a special way of looking beyond all the
pain or doubt and finding a person who can learn
and become anything they want to be. You have
a special way of helping people to make them
feel better, by not giving up on anybody. You except
people no matter what they did wrong. When I'm
around you I feel like I have no problems. You
always find a way to help somebody and that's
what is unique about you.

Clifford
8-202   14

Dear Mrs. B you make me feel good when I sad thats why I love you.
love scipio
SCIPIO
2/07

I ♥ You thank you for Helping me rite I ♥ mis i shapy Beacas you let me cauler LOVE KAYLee
Age 6

2/1/13

Dear Ms. Berkovits
I deeply appreciate what you have done for me taught me new vocabulory words. Taught me what to do when I'm angry and in certain situations it makes me feel good when I'm here I really so deeply appreciate it. Thank you

Sincerly Quincy Joseph

7th grade
age:12

Saika   3B
                                   Age: 8
Dear Ms. Fun,

You are the best teacher we ever had.
When it was the first day we came my
dream came true. I started having a new
life. You made every thing better. If you stop
visiting your children, we will forget you.
We know that will not happen.

                          Your Child,
                          Saika

Ibrahim   June 2000

Ms. B you have teached A lot of thing
to me. you had teached me math a lot
and on my tests I'v got good grades the scores
are. two 70 70 80 90 on my tests you made
my feel smart and happy I very happy threw
the years. I rember when you danced a round
the tables you made my brain very smater
and I love you very mush. and you are
very lovely I will feel sad becuse are
going away for a long time I will
mise you evey Day thank for ms B

         love Ibrahim

                          3rd Grade
                          9 years old just.

Dear Mrs. Berkowitz e'inre
you were + still are
the best person I ever
met So I will never
forget you (even If I am
married I still won't forget
you) I Just know I ♡ U !!

Sincerely,
Ness

STORYTELLING AS A TOOL

Children love to hear a good story and storytelling is an excellent teaching tool. Here is a favorite of mine,[3] which highlights how one woman was able to turn every adverse situation into something positive. Children love it for its ingenuity and humor. They also love that the bad guy gets punished and the good woman gets rewarded.

> *Once there was a monster. His name was The Ugsome Thing.*
> *He was round and fat and had long, ugly, twisted teeth. He*
> *lived in a castle and had many servants who worked for him*
> *day and night. They had to clean his castle, cook his food, till*
> *his fields, and take care of his sheep and cows. Though they*
> *worked so hard, The Ugsome Thing didn't pay them a penny as*
> *wages. He had all the servants he needed except for a washer-*
> *woman to wash and iron his clothes, and he often went dirty*
> *and smelly.*
>
> *The monster had magical powers. He could make anyone be-*
> *come his servant if he made them lose their temper.*
>
> *One day, as he was walking through the village, he saw a cot-*
> *tage garden with the whitest clothes he had ever seen hanging*
> *on the line.*

---

3   "The Ugsome Thing," first published by the BBC in 1977.

"Great," he said. "I know just the thing to make the washer-woman lose her temper and make her my servant. And without waiting a moment, he took his scissors and cut the line, and the snow-white clothes fell to the ground and got dirty. "I can't wait to see the washerwoman lose her temper!" he said.

Just then, the washerwoman came out of her cottage. She saw the clothes lying on the ground, but instead of losing her temper, she said, "Well, well, well. The chimney has been smoking this morning and I'm sure some ashes have fallen on my clothes. How lucky that the line broke this morning and not on any other." She gathered up the dirty clothes and took them to the wash-house, singing as she went.

The Ugsome Thing was very angry but soon thought of another thing to make her lose her temper. So the next day, he visited the woman again and saw that she had milked her cow. The milk was in a pail in the dairy. The wicked Ugsome Thing turned her milk sour. Soon the woman came out of her house. When she saw what had happened, she said, "Well, well, well, I'll have to make the milk into cream cheese. It'll be a treat for my grandchildren. They love cream cheese with their scones and they're coming for tea today. How lucky the milk turned sour today and not on any other!"

The Ugsome Thing was very angry. He gnashed his long, gnarled teeth but soon thought of something else to make the woman lose her temper. The next day, he stretched a piece of string across the woman's stairs, hoping she would trip and fall. "That will surely make her very, very angry," he said. The old woman did trip. She did fall and hurt her knee and had to hop on one leg to the dairy to milk her cow.

"Well, well, well," she said, "I can't do any housework today. I shall lie on the sofa and get on with my patchwork quilt. What a nice change that will be. I may even finish it today. How lucky I am that I tripped today and not on any other."

The Ugsome Thing was very angry and gnashed his ugly teeth but he soon thought of another thing to make the woman lose her temper. The next day he again visited the old woman. He saw her going to the henhouse to collect the eggs. She had three white hens and they each had laid an egg. As she was walking past the apple tree, he flipped a branch in her face and she dropped the bowl and broke the eggs. The Ugsome Thing was delighted. Surely this would make the washerwoman lose her temper. But she said, "Well, well, well. I'll make scrambled eggs for lunch and supper and scrambled eggs are my favorite food. How lucky I am that the eggs broke today and not on another."

The Ugsome Thing was furious. He gnashed his ugly teeth, and made fire come out of his nose because he was very, very angry. He thought of another very, very nasty thing to make the woman lose her temper. He was sure that what he was about to do would work. The woman would lose her temper and he would make her his servant. So he set the old woman's house on fire. The flames shot up the walls and in no time the thatched roof caught fire.

"Well, well, well," the old woman said. "That's the end of my old cottage. I was fond of it, but it was falling to pieces and the roof let in rain, and there were holes in the floor."

When the Ugsome Thing came along he found her baking potatoes in the hot ashes, and handing them around to the village children.

"Have a potato," she said to the Ugsome Thing, holding one out on the point of a stick. It smelled so good that the Ugsome Thing took it and crammed it into his mouth whole because he was so greedy, and he choked and he burst like a balloon, and there was nothing left of him but a piece of greenish shriveled skin. A little boy threw it on the fire, thinking it was an old rag, and it burned with a spluttering yellow flame until it was all gone.

By this time most of the people in the village were lining up to have a baked potato, and while they were waiting, they planned how to help the old woman.

"I'll build the walls of a new cottage," said one.

"I'll make the roof," said another.

"I'll install the windows," said a third.

"I'll paper the walls," said a fourth.

"We'll give her a carpet, curtains, sheets, a blanket, a pillow," said the women. By the time all the potatoes were cooked and eaten, her friends had promised the old woman all she needed for a new cottage.

They all set to work to construct the new cottage. It was not old and tumbledown like the first one. It was dry and comfortable with a sunny porch. The cow had a new shed and the dog a new kennel. The cottage had a beautiful garden with colorful flowers and apple and cherry trees which everybody admired. The old lady used the fruit to bake delicious pastries and regularly invited her friends to join her for tea.

Gratitude Practices

- Teach your child a poem you enjoyed as a child.
- Teach your child a song you like.
- Tell your children stories about your parents and their parents and their parents, going back as far as you can. We all have a great deal to be thankful for to our ancestors, and when we talk about them in this way, we get to feel grateful. Offer prayers of gratitude to those family members who have passed on, and encourage your children to do likewise. This is a good way to honor past family members and at the same time unite present ones.
- Make up a gratitude story or gratitude poem or gratitude song together with your child. Then each of you draw or paint a gratitude picture.

- Go on a "Thankful Hunt." Divide your family into teams and give them a piece of paper with the words *See, Hear, Touch, Smell,* and *Taste* as list headings. The teams hunt for things they can write on their paper—things they can see, hear, touch, smell, and taste that they are grateful for. After the teams have had a few minutes to write the answers, they share their lists with the whole family.

- Give the children a large picture of a tree or have them draw one on a sheet of oak tag. Draw lots of big leaves on the tree. Each day have them write on one of the leaves something they're thankful for that day. Alternatively, you might want to cut out large leaves from the oak tag and have the children pin them onto the tree each day.

CHAPTER 8

Stories of Unintended Consequences

Don't throw stones into the well from which you have drunk.

Bava Kama 92b

A person must show appreciation to the source from which he derived pleasure.

Bereishis Rabbah 79

BACK ON TRACK

Acknowledging someone from whom you've benefited can have astounding results. This applies even to simply thanking a person who is just doing his job.

A young religious fellow traveling on a train in Israel got off at the last stop. He walked to the front of the platform and stopped by the conductor's cab. "Thank you," he said to the surprised man.

"I've worked for thirty years driving trains," the conductor responded. "No one has ever thanked me before."

He was so touched that the religious-looking fellow had taken the trouble to acknowledge him that he engaged him in conversation, during which he asked questions about the way he was dressed, and about his lifestyle. The answers piqued the driver's interest and he was moved to find out more about religious people and their way of life.

Eventually, he went on to study at a Talmudical college and became observant.[1]

Two words, sincerely expressed, led to a truly meaningful outcome.

THE SOLDIER AND THE TRUCK DRIVER

Separated from his platoon, a young Israeli soldier lay at the side of the road, slowly bleeding out. After what seemed like an eternity, a truck pulled up beside him. The driver, who had noticed the wounded soldier, emerged from the vehicle, hastily took off his shirt, and used it to make a life-saving tourniquet. He loaded the soldier into the back of his truck and rushed him to a trauma hospital. Moments from death when found, the soldier slowly regained his strength, and the day came when he was ready to be reunited with his family.

He and his parents wanted, more than anything else, to be able to give thanks to the truck driver. So they placed an ad in the newspaper: "If you were the angel disguised as a truck driver, please contact us. We would like to pay you a visit and express our gratitude." After a few weeks, the family received a phone call from a woman who identified herself as the mother of the good Samaritan.

The soldier and his parents took a taxi to the truck driver's humble home. When they got there, they rang the bell, and the door was opened by a middle-aged woman. Two mothers—one the mother of a hero soldier, and the other the mother of the hero truck driver—gazed upon each other's faces. The truck driver's mother almost fainted as she exclaimed, "I never thought I'd see you again!"

"Again?" the soldier's mother repeated, puzzled. "I never met you before in my life."

The truck driver's mother then proceeded to remind her of their encounter twenty-one years earlier.

"We were seated next to each other in an obstetrician's office. I saw no value in bringing another child into this dangerous, difficult world. You reached out to me and spent the better part of an hour trying to convince me about the sanctity of every life, of every Jewish soul. You

---

1   I heard this story in a Torah class given by Shira Smiles.

tried to persuade me to keep the child, explaining that if God blessed me with the pregnancy, the child would be born with a specific purpose. Not one Jewish soul is born into this world unless it was to make a profound difference in another person's life, you assured me.

"I was touched by your interest in me, a total stranger, and I decided to have my baby—who turned out to be my only child, whom I love with all my heart—my son the truck driver.

"You saved my son's life before he was born. He saved your son's life before he could bleed to death. I now see, more clearly than ever, how your words of twenty-one years ago were true beyond all bounds of truth. No soul is born into this world unless he or she can affect the soul of another."

THE PIZZA MAN'S DOUGH

I've often noticed how grateful people tend to be more generous, more giving of their time and money. This was true of the Pizza Man, an immigrant who came to these shores to earn a living. He owned a tiny pizza joint with only a small table and two chairs, on the outskirts of Boro Park.

One day, a Muslim man who occasionally patronized the pizzeria, came by and asked for a three-hundred-dollar loan that he needed for rent. The Pizza Man gave him the money.

A week later, three Muslim thugs accosted the Pizza Man. Just as this was happening, who should appear but the man who had borrowed the money! He scared the thugs and they ran away.

"How come you were here at just this moment?" the Pizza Man asked him, shaken.

"I came," said the Muslim, "to pay back the money you loaned me." Coincidence? I think not.

INSTANT RECALL

In a lecture, Rabbi Paysach Krohn related that he travels a lot and is frequently in airports. One day, he was about to board the plane when he saw an airport security man walking rapidly in his direction.

"He's looking at me. Am I in some kind of trouble?" Rabbi Krohn anxiously wondered.

The security man approached. "Sir," he said, "is this your mobile phone?"

"I didn't even know it was missing," Rabbi Krohn replied. "How did you get it?"

The security agent said, "When you went through security, your mobile phone was left in the bin."

"How did you know this is my phone? Hundreds of people go through security!" Rabbi Krohn exclaimed.

The security guard answered, "After you went through, you turned around and said, 'Thank you.' Not many say thank you; in fact, most people must think we're simply a necessary nuisance. Your saying thank you made such an impression on me that I made it a point to look at your face, and it registered in my mind—so it wasn't difficult to recognize you."

Amazing, isn't it? Because Rabbi Krohn turned around and said thank you, he got his cell phone back!

"Imagine," he concluded, "I would have lost all my numbers if I hadn't said thank you!"

ENHANCED VISION

I heard a story about a mother who encouraged her nine-year-old daughter to do a *chessed* (kind deed) and visit a sixty-three-year-old blind woman who had moved into the next building. Being shy, the girl was reluctant, but her mother kept encouraging her. "Try it once and see how you feel. You might find it's not so difficult, and it'll mean so much to the blind lady."

The girl visited the woman every week and read books to her. A beautiful relationship developed between them. One day, the blind lady told the girl that in two years' time she would be able to see because of a new technology that could restore her eyesight. She said she didn't have the money to pay for it, but when she reached the age of sixty-five, she would get Social Security benefits and be able to have the surgery.

The following day, at school, the girl went from class to class telling the students she needed money to help the blind lady to see. She collected eighty-three one-dollar bills and put them in a tattered envelope. She accompanied the woman to an Orthodox Jewish ophthalmologist and gave him the tattered envelope with the eighty-three singles. The ophthalmologist performed the surgery, and the blind woman regained her eyesight.

When the mother of the girl found out, she went to the ophthalmologist and promised to pay him the true price of the surgery in monthly installments.

"Absolutely not!" the ophthalmologist replied.

He removed the tattered envelope with the eighty-three one-dollar bills from his pocket and said, "I keep this envelope in my pocket and carry it wherever I go. Whenever I feel a little down, I take it out and look at it. It restores my faith in humanity."

A THOUGHT TO CHEW ON

When Rabbi Avigdor Miller was hospitalized, a nurse came to his bedside carrying a small dish of water.

"What is this for?" asked Rabbi Miller.

"It's for your teeth," answered the nurse.

"But my teeth don't come out," Rabbi Miller replied.

The nurse was astounded that the rabbi, who was in his nineties, did not wear dentures.

"Why do you think you have all your teeth?" she asked.

To which Rabbi Miller responded, "Every time I brush my teeth, I say, 'Thank you, Hashem. You gave me food and you gave me incisors and molars to grind and chew my food. Thank you so much for these wonderful teeth and for the digestive juices and enzymes that help me digest and absorb my food.'

"I have said this twice a day—morning and night—for ninety years. It is in this merit that I still have my teeth."

Gratitude Practices

- Ask yourself: "From whom have I benefited but not acknowledged adequately or at all?" Then find a way to show your appreciation.
- Make a scrapbook of your favorite gratitude sayings. Perhaps begin it with Melody Beattie:[2] "Gratitude can turn a meal into a feast, a house into a home, a stranger into a friend." Contemplate the meaning of each, then write down your thoughts about it and discuss it with a friend or family member. Read the entries in your scrapbook from time to time, perhaps at the beginning of every week, or whenever suits you. Don't fall into the morass of forgetfulness, which is a major cause of people's lack of gratitude. Regularly reading your scrapbook will help you remember the many reasons why you should be grateful.

---

2   *Gratitude: Affirming the Good Things in Life*, MJF Books, 1992.

CHAPTER 9

Glimpses into My Journal

*To appreciate beauty, to find the best
in others, to give one's self...this is
to have succeeded.*

Ralph Waldo Emerson

I STARTED KEEPING a gratitude journal many years ago, hoping it would increase my awareness of the blessings, both large and small, I received on a daily basis, and ultimately make me a more grateful person. I made up my mind not to let even one day go by without noticing and recording something that happened that made me happy: the train arrived almost as soon as I got to the platform; it was raining but I had remembered to take my umbrella; I woke up way too early, which gave me only four hours of sleep, but I was able to use this time to reach family members who lived abroad in England and Israel on the phone; the milk for my tea hadn't gone sour though it frequently spoiled in my fridge after only a few days; I received a real snail-mail letter from a friend, a pleasant change from the bills and never-ending junk mail.

I began with just one or two journal entries daily and wrote down whatever things I was grateful for that spontaneously entered my mind. It became a daily ritual. I would make myself a cup of tea first thing in the morning and, sipping it, would spend a few minutes writing in my journal. I carefully chose the book I wanted to use for my journal entries—the right size, the right spacing of the lines, and an attractive cover. At the top of the page I entered the date and time each day.

With the passage of time, an increasing number of things for which to be grateful kept popping into my head. I found myself going about my day feeling happier and more optimistic. When something untoward happened—for example, the elevator in my building breaking down for the umpteenth time—I found myself saying, "There's a bonus here. I get to walk up and down the stairs and the exercise will do me good."

Keeping a gratitude journal helps me stay positive during my day. As I focus on things for which to be grateful, I feel abundantly blessed. I find myself giving larger tips to the hairdresser, taxi driver, and restaurant waiter or waitress. When I feel happy and blessed, I want to make other people happy, too.

Day by day, week by week, I find more and more things to be grateful for, and this puts me in an upbeat frame of mind. I feel more alive more of the time, more energetic, more connected to myself, more connected to other people, and more productive. This is not to say I never experience a low mood—we all do at times—but when this happens, it generally doesn't last as long as it used to, because underlying everything there is gratitude. With time, when I would lie in bed at night, I began to focus my attention on all the things that had gone right during my day, and I found I was falling asleep more easily.

Keeping a gratitude journal changed my focus and literally changed my life.

It is now my pleasure to share some of my journal entries with you.

BE OPEN TO WHAT THE DAY BRINGS

The most amazing thing happened to me today. I got up especially early to go swimming. The bus came just as I reached the bus stop. *How fortunate I am*, I said to myself.

When I got off the bus, I started walking in the direction of the Kings Bay Y, where the swimming pool was housed. On the pavement in front of me were scores of pigeons huddled together, busily pecking at seeds. Some kind person had gotten up early to feed the birds. I found myself feeling grateful to that person for having afforded me this beautiful sight. The pigeons were not the only ones to benefit from this kind person, I also benefited because I saw the amazing spectacle of the pigeons peacefully pecking at the seeds, each bird knowing that there was enough food to go around without having to fight for it.

When I got to the Y, there was a sign on the door: "POOL CLOSED FOR EMERGENCY REPAIRS." I can't say I wasn't disappointed. I had so much looked forward to going swimming for some time, but had been unable to fit it into my busy schedule. Surprisingly, I did not find myself reacting with anger. I thought it would have been nice if they had sent out an email to inform us of the closure. I did not bemoan the fact that I had gotten up especially early for nothing.

Walking back to the bus stop, I was thinking about the *Modeh Ani* prayer, how when I say it with a smile it makes me feel so happy. And at that moment I found myself feeling grateful for my tongue and teeth that enable me to verbalize the prayer; for the fact that I was born into a religious family and received a solid Jewish education; for my first-grade teacher who taught me to read Hebrew so I'm able to pray in the holy language, and for being part of the *am hanivchar*, God's chosen people.

And then the most amazing thing happened. I was on the bus returning home and noticed that the woman sitting opposite me had dropped the wire from her cell phone. I pointed it out to her. She was so grateful, she thanked me profusely not merely with words, but she actually bowed her head. As I stood to get off the bus, she shoved a dollar bill into my hand. I shook my head and said, "No, no," but she insisted. "Take it, take it, it's yours," she said, and then she shoved another crumpled-up note into my hand. Again I objected, but she would not take no for an answer.

When I got off the bus, I noticed she had actually given me three dollar bills. I thought, *how blessed I am that the pool was closed this morning!* Had it been open and had I gone swimming, I would not have had this encounter with this most unusual woman.

I asked her for her name as I got off the bus.

"Tassie," she said.

Thank you, Tassie, for teaching me an important lesson in gratitude, that even for the most minuscule benefit we receive from a person we need to thank wholeheartedly.

I keep these dollar bills in my possession and from time to time I take them in my hand and think: *How blessed I am to have met this remarkable woman!*

THANK YOU TO MY GREAT-GRANDMOTHER

The other day, I was reflecting upon the good qualities I inherited from my great-grandmother, Rebbetzin Shaindel Wesel, who was a striking example of someone who lived with gratitude through her many deeds of *chessed.*

I am thankful for my love of gardening, which she passed on to my mother, who passed it on to me. I was not fortunate enough to know her, but my mother told me that she had a little garden and she grew cucumbers which she pickled and sold to gourmet restaurants. She also grew strawberries, making sure to have the first ones of the season. Because they were the first fruits, she was able to command a hefty price for them. In her later years she became sick, but she didn't stop gardening. She carried a small stool as she moved around in the little garden, sitting down as much as possible while working. With the money she earned she helped a number of poor families who came to her on a weekly basis, seeking assistance for food for Shabbos.

"On Thursday evenings, between the hours of six and ten, no one was allowed in the kitchen," my mother told me. It was then that eighteen poor women came to my great-grandmother's for their weekly money for Shabbos food. My great-grandmother was extremely sensitive to the feelings of others. She wanted to avoid any embarrassment on the part of these women.

When my great-grandfather, Rabbi Benzion Wesel, built a new shul, his gratitude knew no bounds upon its completion, but his joy was marred by the fact that he didn't have any more money for the *ner tamid* (the special light that remains lit day and night in front of the holy ark where the Torah scrolls are housed).

"Everybody has given their utmost," he told my great-grandmother. "I can't ask them to donate any more."

"Don't worry," she said, as she went into the adjoining room. A minute later she reappeared with a white cloth bundle in her hands. "Here's your *ner tamid*," she said, as she opened the bundle, displaying silver coins she had collected specifically for that purpose. "Ever since you said you wanted to build a new shul, I collected and set aside these silver coins for the *ner tamid*."

They worked so beautifully together as a team and their joy was now complete.

POTENTIAL

On my way to work one morning, I was waiting for the bus beside a large empty corner lot on the border of Bedford-Stuyvesant and Williamsburg. It was cold, with solid gray skies—an inauspicious, dull morning with the kind of gloomy, gray-white sky that usually precedes snow. It began to drizzle, followed by heavier rain. The forecast had not mentioned rain, and I hadn't brought my umbrella. I didn't want my hair to get frizzy.

Ages passed. The bus didn't come. Then two things happened. I looked down at the pavement and saw a little silvery something covered by dirt. I bent down to look closer. It was a dime. I took it in my hand, cleaned it, and put it in my pocket.

Sometimes, we come across a treasure which we don't recognize as such because it's covered by dirt. I was thinking about my students. *Every child is a treasure*, I thought, sometimes hard to see, because of the outer layer of "dirt" such as character flaws or disruptive, oppositional, defiant behaviors. But if we patiently work at cleaning away the "dirt," we will find the treasure that each child is.

The bus still didn't come. I turned around, looked behind me, and saw a vacant lot. There was a large sign in bold black Hebrew letters which read, "Here there will be built, with the help of God, a synagogue for prayer and Torah study, and a ritual bath."

How interesting, I said to myself. *This vacant lot is more than just a yard strewn with litter and rubble. It has the potential of becoming a holy place.*

And then I thought, *the empty lots are the children in school who are not succeeding. They will remain unsuccessful unless we shift our gaze. We need to see them with new eyes, stop seeing them as failures, and focus on who they can become.* When we begin to believe in them, encourage them, and imbue them with feelings of self-worth, they will begin to believe in themselves and actualize their hidden potential.

ON MY WAY TO WORK

One cold morning I noticed a little old lady with a very wrinkled face sitting on a low stool outside the subway station. It was difficult to tell her age. Clad in black tatty clothes with a black kerchief on her head, she looked forlorn, so I put my hand in my pocket, pulled out a ten-dollar bill and gave it to her. Immediately, my mood was uplifted. I felt good that I had started my day by helping someone. I came to school and shared this with the school secretary, and she told me the following story.

"Years ago," she said, "I used to collect money for a yeshiva, going door to door. A lady gave me a dollar. I said, 'Thank you so much,' to which the lady replied, '*You're* thanking me? I need to thank you! You enabled me to do a good deed.'"

Whenever we are able to help someone, even in a very small way, we should thank the person whom we helped because they enabled us to become a better human being.

GIVING

Sometimes we pass beggars in the street and walk straight on, questioning whether they are genuinely poor. But the Torah says, "*Paso'ach tiftach es yadecha*—Open, open your hand."[1] Why the double expression? Perhaps we can learn from the repetition that we should give, and, after we've given, we should give again—that is to say, we should continue to give, give, and then give more.[2] Don't rest and say, "I'm not giving this time, I've already given."

---

1   *Devarim* 15:8.
2   See *Rashi* on this *pasuk*, who is quoting this from the *Sifri*, *Re'eh* 116.

Another explanation might be: Give until you feel you've given, until it makes a dent in your finances. Thank the recipients of your generosity for having given you the opportunity to be generous, and thank God for the opportunity He's given you to be a giver.

DETOUR FOR JOY

Some people are absolutely amazing! They go out of their way to do you a favor and then they thank you for the gift they say *you* gave them!

I met Barbara, an attractive woman in her sixties, with short curly gray hair, at a writing conference in Pennsylvania, in the summer of 2018. Barbara is a fascinating woman. She's won commendations for her poetry and her photography; she's published several children's books and makes beautiful dolls. She showed me a three-foot stuffed moose she created. She has lots of different clothes for it, which she herself stitched. She keeps it in her SUV as her travel companion.

When the conference was over, Barbara asked me how I was planning to get home. I said, "I live in Brooklyn. I'll take the bus to the Port Authority Terminal, and from there, the subway."

Barbara said, "I'll take you."

This meant that she'd be driving three hours out of her way to take me to Brooklyn, and then she'd have to drive back to New Jersey! When I told her it was out of the question, she said, "People have done some nice things for me. I don't feel like I'm putting myself out. It's what I do." I relented. During the trip we talked about lots of things: about life, about feelings, about family hurts, about what gives us joy.

"I have a lot of sadness and I could easily dwell in it," she said, "but I've made a choice to live in joy. Why not do something so that somebody else can share that joy? Why not spread it?"

"It's admirable," I said. "You're recreating yourself; you're recreating your life. It takes courage to let go of the hurt."

"All we have is now," Barbara said. "I try to make the best of *now*. Many years ago, I heard Oprah say, 'Write three things a day for which you're grateful.' I wrote a page a day for two years! It taught me to have a positive attitude."

"There's so much I can learn from you," I said. "It's not an accident that God brought the two of us together."

"There's a life lesson in whatever is thrown your way," Barbara said. "I'm so glad I am who I am. I don't hold a grudge. That's what's made my life so well worth living."

As we crossed the Verrazano Bridge, Barbara got excited. "I used to sail my boat here for twenty-five years but had to give it up due to ill health. Returning after many years brings back fond memories and gives me a thrill."

"This has been really delightful," she said, as we arrived at my house and shared a parting hug. "I have to thank you," she added, "because *you* have given *me* a gift."

As she turned to head back to New Jersey, I called after her. "You shine the light in the dark places. You don't keep it for yourself. You pass it on to others."

I ENCOUNTER THE PIGEON LADY AND MAKE A NEW FRIEND

I came out of the bank, crossed Nostrand Avenue, and walked by the large municipal parking lot at Flatbush Junction. It was ten minutes to 1:00 p.m. on a Friday in April. There was a slight breeze in the balmy air and the sun had finally broken through the clouds. Standing outside the tall iron fencing was an elderly lady wearing a flimsy red cotton jacket, gray polyester skirt, and a red knitted hat. She carried a large bag of sliced white bread in her hand and was throwing bits of bread over the fence. There must have been thirty or forty pigeons crowding together, pecking away.

"Hello," I smiled, "do you often feed the pigeons?"

"Almost every day," she replied, looking me in the face with her soft dark brown eyes. "The police threatened they'd give me a ticket," she went on, "but I said, 'You ate breakfast today, didn't you? Well, these are also God's creatures. They have to eat, too!'"

"You're right," I said. "It's nice of you to feed them."

"'They spread disease,' the policeman said. But they don't spread no disease, they don't have AIDS or 'tumorcolosis.' Besides, look," she said, turning her bag to me, "it's only eighty-nine cents for a large loaf. I spend three dollars each week feeding the pigeons."

"You're a kind lady," I said.

"My mother had ten children. They're all gone now except for me. My oldest sister died last year. She was 103! I don't know why God kept me here, but he must have His reasons."

"I'm one of eight," I offered.

"Really?" she said, her voice full of surprise.

"Yes. I come from England."

"I love England," she said. "I've been there ten times. One of my sisters used to live there. She's gone, but my nephew's still there. We went to Madeira together, that's in Portugal. And another year we went to Wales. I love London."

"And where are you from?" I asked.

"I'm from Jamaica," she said. "My mother was a very special woman, one of the best creatures that God ever made. She died in 1966. I have her picture on my dresser. I used to visit her often. One day I brought her some lunch—fish and two green bananas. When I gave it to her she divided the fish into two portions, put half in one dish and half in another, and put one banana in each dish.

"'Mother,' I said, 'what are you doing? This is your lunch.'"

"'There's some child out there who has no food,' my mother said. 'I'm putting it aside for that child.'

"And then, a thin, pale lady came by. 'How are you?' my mother asked her. 'Have you had anything to eat today?'

"'No,' said the haggard woman.

"'Well, here is some food for you, then. I'm about to have my lunch. Please, won't you join me?'

"And that was my mother, always looking to help others."

"Now I understand why you feed the pigeons, even though you surely don't have money to spare. How old are you?" I asked.

"Guess," she said.

"Sixty," I ventured.

"Try again."

"Sixty-five."

"Try again."

"Seventy."

"More than that. I'm eighty-five! I'm very lucky. God has been good to me. I have my health; I have enough food. God takes such good care of us," she said, her voice full of gratitude, "so I take care of His creatures, too."

NOBODY'S BIRTHDAY

One day I bought my sister a fragrant long-stemmed red rose with beautiful silky petals. It wasn't her birthday. It was just an ordinary day. As I walked down the street toward her house, a passerby said, "Happy birthday."

"It isn't my birthday," I said. "I just thought I'd give my sister a flower."

I continued on my way to the local library to pick up a book. There I met an acquaintance.

"Somebody loves you," she said.

"Yes," I replied, pointing upward. "He loves me and my friends love me and members of my family love me—and Someone loves you, too," I said, and smiled. She smiled back at me as we said goodbye to one another.

When we feel blessed, we feel gratitude, and when we feel gratitude, we feel happy, and the joy we exude often leads to positive interactions with people we encounter as we go through our day.

ENCOUNTER WITH A CAR SERVICE DRIVER

I met an interesting car service driver named Bob, who proudly told me about his daughter, mother of four, who has an artificial leg.

"When she was born, the bone in one of her legs was missing," he said. "She could have had countless surgeries before age fourteen, or an artificial leg. After much deliberation, we opted for the prosthesis.

"It hasn't stopped her from living a full life," he added. "She goes skiing, running, cycling, and also plays different sports. She works with handicapped children, including some with autism. Having overcome a handicap, she understands handicapped children better than many of us do."

I was impressed with what a full life she leads, allowing absolutely nothing to deter her from pursuing her many interests and working on a daily basis, using her intelligence, talents, and skill, not to mention extraordinary patience, to improve the life of physically and mentally challenged children.

MAKING OUR DAYS COUNT

I woke up this morning with a question on my mind: Do we count our days or do we make our days count?

I know a number of people who, beyond a certain age, get ill at ease with the onset of their birthday. It seems to remind them that they are getting older, and this is something many people fear. They fear possible impending poor health, loss of physical beauty, loss of physical prowess, and possible loss of independence. More than anything, they have a hard time facing their own mortality. But we are finite beings, and one day we will die. The only infinite is God—who was, is, and always will be. So, we might as well get comfortable with the idea that our time on this earth is temporary.

Instead of counting our days and fretting about time passing, let's make our days count. Let us live each day fully. Let us not fritter away the time we have allotted to us. Let us make each day meaningful, each day a day of personal spiritual growth, a day of fulfilling God's will, of enhancing our relationships, of finding inner peace; a day when we see beauty in ourselves as well as in all the people we encounter, a day when we slow down and pay attention to the beauty in the world. There is so much beauty around us and in us. We are, after all, created in the image of God. We possess a Divine soul. In our dealings with people, family members, colleagues, and acquaintances, let us look for that Divine spark. Let us see the beauty in the order of the world, testifying to the magnificence of the Creator. Let us be filled with awe and, above all, let us be filled with gratitude.

The moment we feel gratitude, everything changes. We are humbled, we feel favored, we feel indebted. We feel we have been given so many gifts, not because we deserve them, but purely by the grace of God. When we cultivate a grateful heart, we ignite the Divine spark within us, and enhance our connection to the Almighty. And, finally, feeling grateful makes us happier, as we realize how abundantly we are blessed.

A HOLOCAUST SURVIVOR SPEAKS

I gave a Torah class the other day. An elderly woman related that she was a Holocaust survivor.

"All I dreamed about," she said, "was that one day I would be able to hold a whole loaf of bread in my hands."

How many of us are grateful that we can hold a whole loaf of bread in our hands? Or are we unhappy because there are still things we don't have that we want? Being ungrateful is a major character flaw. We can change. We can train our eyes to see the good in our situation, in our family, in our lot in life.

THE SCIENCE FAIR

There was an impressive science fair at school today. Students from kindergarten through eighth grade presented their projects. The numerous displays indicated that a great deal of learning had taken place. There was excitement and upbeat energy everywhere. I complimented the science teacher for the wonderful job she had done, acknowledging that it must have been a tremendous amount of work to put it all together. She told me she had been doing it for five years and never got a word of recognition, neither from the other teachers nor from the principal.

"On Monday, all the criticism will come in," she said. "They will tell me this wasn't good enough, that wasn't good enough, this wasn't done right, that could have been improved upon. You don't do it to get thanks, I know; it's been like this every year!" She was trying hard to hold back her tears. "Thank you for thanking me. You're the first one ever to do so."

"To work so hard and not to be acknowledged, to be taken for granted, must be very hurtful." I gave her a hug and she thanked me again for caring.

Isn't it sad? It takes no time to say thank you nor does it cost anything, yet many people are loath to express appreciation.

LOOKING UP

In the news today I read, "Oldest man in recorded history dies at 116, in Japan."

Jiroemon Kimura, a 116-year-old former post-office worker, was born in 1897, the same year as the aviator Amelia Earhart, and the year that Britain's Queen Victoria marked her Diamond Jubilee. Kimura died of natural causes in Kyoto. He was recognized by *Guinness* as the oldest man documented in history and was dubbed "the last known man to live across three centuries." Kimura would greet almost every visitor from abroad with the English phrase he learned: "Thank you very much, you are very kind."

Kimura attributed his longevity to getting out in the sunlight. I like to think of this in a figurative way—that he always looked at the bright side of things. Just as the sun is bright, so too did he focus on what is full of light, the bright side, the silver lining in every cloud.

There are clouds in everybody's life, times when life looks tough due to sickness, problematic relationships, financial difficulties, natural disasters, or challenges in raising children. We have a choice—to focus on what isn't right or to "look up toward the sun" and attempt to find some good in every situation. When things are tough, when we are being challenged in life, we can complain about it or we can ask ourselves what lessons we can learn from this experience.

"I'm always looking up toward the sky. That's how I am," Kimura said. Looking up toward the sky—what does that mean? For me it means looking up toward the heavens, God's abode. Perhaps Kimura was saying, *I see God in every situation. I know God is love, God is mercy, God wants to reward us for our good deeds. Moreover, when we are with God, we are never alone.*

What a comforting thought. Many people experience existential loneliness, for even when we are deeply connected to someone else there is always a part of us that remains not understood. But when we are with God we are never alone. "*Shivisi Hashem l'negdi samid*—I put God before me all the time."[3]

---

3   *Tehillim* 16:8.

Kimura lived to 116. He experienced loneliness because when one reaches a ripe old age, one sees friends and family members die, one after the other. He could have wallowed in his loneliness, complained, been grumpy, but he didn't. Instead, he said, "I am always looking up toward the sky."

HOW ARE YOU?

One of the teachers at school this morning asked me how I am. I replied, "This is the day that God made, let us rejoice and be happy on it![4] It's a new day, a new opportunity for growth, for giving and receiving love, for enjoying the beauty in nature that God created for us to enjoy."

I felt happy, alive, awake, and ever so grateful. I shared this with other teachers during the day and watched as they smiled and thanked me for opening their eyes and hearts to the gift of each new day.

BLESSINGS

I woke up this morning feeling wonderfully blessed: I have a job to go to, a supportive family, friends, colleagues, and acquaintances. I can breathe without difficulty. I can go and come as I please. I live in a democratic country which permits me to have freedom of worship and freedom of speech. There is an abundance of Torah classes in my neighborhood and many more classes available on the Internet or the phone. I can go to the library and borrow books that inspire me. I have many opportunities to get involved with other people's lives, to listen to them and give them hope and encouragement when needed, and countless opportunities to give charity.

This is only a fraction of what I can accomplish today, tomorrow, this week, next week, throughout the year. I have so many reasons to be grateful!

EARLY MORNING SWIM

I went swimming early this morning; women's swimming is from 7:00 to 8:00 a.m. I took the B44 bus at Nostrand Avenue. During the

---

4   *Tehillim* 118:24.

fifteen-minute bus ride, I entertained myself by softly reciting things for which I am grateful.

"I'm grateful that I wasn't stung by a mosquito today or stung by a bee." (I'm highly allergic, so it's really important that they stay away from me.) I continued, "I'm grateful that I wasn't a thalidomide baby, that I'm not diabetic, that I know how to swim." (It took me ages to learn—it was six months before I could even float because, fearful to let go, I kept one foot on the bottom of the pool all the time!)

My list continued: "I'm grateful that I woke up this morning fully in control of myself, that I didn't listen to the voice that said, 'Why don't you just stay in bed a little longer?' I'm grateful that I have fingernails and toenails. That when I accidentally cut myself, skin grows back and the body amazingly heals itself." I was grateful that it wasn't too hot (although the prediction for the day was 90 degrees with high humidity and a real-feel temperature of 95). There was shade on one side of the street and a gentle breeze blowing. I was grateful that the pool wasn't crowded. (I hate swimming in crowded pools.) I was grateful that the steam room and sauna were working, which is not always the case.

Later, I had to go to Manhattan. I didn't get a seat on the subway coming back; however, though the trains were packed, we weren't as squashed as sardines, something I was extremely grateful for. (I hate it when bodies are pressed against bodies in rush-hour travel.) I love to relax with the morning newspaper crossword puzzle, but they didn't deliver it in Brooklyn today. However, I was fortunate because I was able to get a copy on Eighth Avenue in Manhattan, and I was grateful for this, too.

THE RICHEST PERSON IN THE WORLD

While descending the stairs to the subway platform, I saw a homeless war veteran sitting on the stairs. I'm grateful that I am among the givers and, thank God, not one who is dependent on the alms of others. Later that day I saw a blind man tapping his cane as he slowly navigated the street. I'm the richest person in the world. I have my eyesight. If you were blind, God forbid, wouldn't you give five million dollars, even considerably more, to regain your sight? I also saw a lady propelling herself in a wheelchair. Thank You, God, I can walk. What a gift! I saw a woman walking with a walker and it made me acknowledge how fortunate I am that I don't need one.

ABOVE TIME AND BEYOND SPACE

I used to teach teachers, social workers, school counselors, and psychologists in the After School Professional Development Program of the New York City Department of Education. From time to time, I encounter Gail, who is now a retired high school teacher, who attended some of these classes. Over the years, we've become great friends. She is very inspirational, loving nothing more than learning Torah and doing *chessed*. Always growing spiritually, she has attended *shiurim* (Torah classes) several times a week for many years. When she is not studying Torah, she is busy helping people in various ways. She regularly visits people in two nursing homes, shops for an elderly widow, and packs Shabbos food packages for needy families.

I invited her to share her thoughts about the essence and nature of gratitude.

"Wherever you are," she began, "it's an opportunity to express gratitude to Hashem. Gratitude transcends time and space. It's a 24/7 connection to Hashem. His bountiful blessings are manifest—a train arrives, a bus comes, you find something you misplaced. Expressing gratitude is the essence of being a Jew.

"I'm so grateful to Hashem for giving me the parents and siblings I had. They taught me important values; they taught me how to prioritize what's important and what's not. I became a *baalas teshuvah*. The rabbi with whom I became close saw a jewel in every Jew. I was blessed to be privy to his wisdom and teachings, and to be immersed in a religious environment, which helped me gain a deep understanding of what's important in life and what life means. Hashem was clearing the path for me."

HAPPY WITH ONE'S LOT

Early this morning I went to the grocery store. I thanked the young fellow who served me and wished him a good day.

"You have a better one," he said.

Some people are so happy with their lot that they wish others to be equally happy, equally blessed; they wish them to have even more than they have. The opposite is true of those who are jealous or envious: If they don't have something, they don't want others to have it, either.

THANKFUL FOR THINGS THAT GO MY WAY

One morning I tried to phone my sister in Israel and couldn't get a dial tone. I didn't understand why, because the previous day the phone was in perfect order.

I had an important phone call to make to London. It was my sister-in-law's birthday and I knew it would mean a lot to her if I remembered it. Perhaps it's the battery, I thought, but no, there was nothing to alert me that I needed a new one. I checked to make sure all the wires were plugged in properly. What a nuisance. I'd have to call in a repair person to identify the problem. It would cost me eighty dollars just for him to come out and I didn't even know if he could fix it. Besides, I didn't have time to wait around.

I have a cell phone but I can't make overseas calls from it. I called a friend on my cell phone and asked her to call my landline to see whether I could receive calls. And lo and behold, I could. And then the dial tone came back as suddenly as it had disappeared. My frustration was turned into tremendous gratitude. Was this God's way of telling me I need to be more grateful for all the myriads of things that do go my way, on a regular daily basis?

BE THE FIRST TO GREET

I awoke one morning with the words of our Sages on my mind: "*Hevei makdim b'shlom kol adam*—Be the first to greet every person."[5] I've been trying to practice this and have observed amazing results. When I greet someone, no matter who it is, with a genuine, sincere smile, nine out of ten times I get a smile back. If it's someone I know, I make sure to impart to them how much I appreciate them. If they've done me a kindness, no matter how long ago, I remind them how much it meant to me

---

5   *Pirkei Avos* 4:15.

and how grateful I still am for it. I'm heartened by the warm smile they give me in return. It's such a joy to see their faces light up.

It occurred to me that *shalom*, besides meaning "hello" and "peace," also means "welfare." Perhaps our Sages are teaching us that not only should we be the first to greet every person, we should also be concerned about their welfare. In other words, we should greet them in a way that makes them feel good, by greeting them with a smile and adding a kind word showing appreciation of who they are. I think when we're told to "greet *every* person" it could also include oneself; namely, we should also be concerned about our own welfare. How can we show that we're concerned about our own welfare? By being concerned about others' welfare, you're also taking care of your own, because what you give out comes back to you. When I smile at people, they smile back at me. It's easy, and it's a good way to strengthen interpersonal relationships.

THE WOMAN WHO BELIEVES IN GIVING BACK

I picked up a local Brooklyn paper and was inspired when I read a short article entitled "Treating Stains and Customers Correctly." The article described a Colombian woman who immigrated to the United States when she was eighteen. She got a job at a dry-cleaning store and learned everything about the trade. Eventually, she opened her own dry-cleaning store in Manhattan, then moved the business to Brooklyn. It was called Bridge Cleaners and Tailors.

This woman believes in giving back, so she collects, cleans, and repairs children's coats and donates them to schools and nonprofit organizations. Should you have a job interview, she will dry-clean your suit free of charge. She expresses her gratitude for the opportunities this country has given her by giving to others.[6]

AT THE SUPERMARKET

I spent my sabbatical year in Jerusalem. One day, I saw a woman standing in front of me on the line at the supermarket looking amazingly happy. I asked her, "What is the secret of happiness?"

---

6   You can read more about her by going to www.bridgecleaners.com.

She said, "I'll answer you with a story. Once there was a woman who had two sons; one worked in agriculture, the other was a potter. Whenever it rained, she was upset for the potter. Whenever the sun shone, she was upset for the farmer. Another woman had two sons—one a farmer, the other a potter. When it rained, she was happy for the farmer; when the sun came out, she was happy for the potter.

"That," she said, "is the secret of happiness."

INSIGHTS

Every occasion when I comprehend something new is cause for celebration, cause for gratitude. I couldn't have understood the material or the concepts without Hashem gracing me with the gift of wisdom and intelligence. There's simply no way I could understand anything were it not for this gift from God.

He makes this gift available to us every moment of every day. The gift of intelligence is always available, it's always there helping us grow intellectually and emotionally. God gives us *chochmah*, *binah*, and *daas* (wisdom, understanding, and knowledge). It is this gift that enables us to have new ideas and new creative insights.

Being blessed with new insights generates tremendous joy in me. It makes me want to sing, renders me more alive, makes me more energized, and elevates my mood. I love to share these insights with others, and this adds not only to my joy but also to theirs. Sharing insights is one of the many ways I connect to people, and when this happens, I go about my day feeling uplifted. And in this uplifted mood more insights pop up and I am blessed. And I am grateful.

Yesterday I left my house early to go to work but didn't get a seat on the train. My trip is at least an hour long—I travel from Brooklyn to Manhattan—and it wasn't easy for me to stand for this length of time. I am recovering from a broken foot and still have pain. I was disappointed that the train was so overcrowded. But all of a sudden, I found I was extremely happy because I realized how grateful I was for all the times I *did* get a seat. This shift in my state of mind happened spontaneously. I didn't deliberately try to look for the good in an untoward situation, hadn't made a special effort to remind myself that every cloud has a silver lining. The transformation or shift of my emotional state from upset to joy came to me as an insight, a veritable gift from God. And I was—and am—so grateful. Insights are such a blessing.

A similar thing happened to me when I lost my phone. It was somewhere in my apartment, but try as I might, I couldn't find it. I went looking in all the places I thought it could be, and some places where I thought it couldn't be, but it didn't show up. One day passed; two days, three. I was really put out, aggravated and annoyed at myself for not having paid attention to where I had put it initially. And then, as if by magic, my upset was suddenly transformed, and I was feeling happy.

What caused this amazing reversal of my emotions was the thought of the tremendous joy I would have when I eventually found it. This thought spontaneously popped into my head, came to me as an insight, once again a gift from God. My heart was filled with gratitude. And then I found it!

HAPPINESS DOES NOT COME FROM MATERIAL GOODS

It's a fallacy to believe that material goods are the key to happiness. Happiness is an attitude. I appreciate what I have, I appreciate who I am, I appreciate the fact that each day affords me new opportunities for personal growth, and I appreciate mistakes I've made because they are my teachers. Hopefully, I learn from my mistakes. I used to castigate myself for making mistakes, but now I ask myself: What lesson can I learn from this experience? I am happier, more self-accepting; more grateful. Being more grateful enhances my health and well-being. It connects me to myself, to people, and to God. When this happens, I feel more energized, more optimistic, less depressed, and less anxious. People who see me in this upbeat frame are drawn toward me, so I am less lonely.

THE HEALING POWER OF EXTENDING ONESELF TO OTHERS

Today I read a story about a woman who got very depressed when her only child left home for college 2,100 miles away. A good friend of hers suggested she start each day by sending a note or card of appreciation to someone she cared about, and to do this for seven days in a row. This woman was in such a deep depression that she had trouble thinking of anything she could appreciate. But each day it got a little easier.

Starting each morning with this ritual, she realized how disconnected and isolated she had become. She soon discovered the healing power of extending herself to others and found that in no time at all this simple gesture of expressing appreciation improved her relationships. She began to feel more connected and by the seventh day her depression lifted.

GRATEFUL THOUGHTS CREATE GOOD FEELINGS

I sat down and spontaneously made a list of things I'm grateful for. I wrote whatever came to my mind without thinking about it, without censoring. I wrote quickly. It took only a couple of minutes, but it put me in a good mood and made me feel positive and strangely more in control of my life.

I went to the library and didn't waste even one moment on the Internet or reading the paper but got right down to editing my manuscript. I know the Internet steals time from writing because there are so many interesting things one can look up, so many distractions that take me away from my work, but after compiling my gratitude list I didn't even go near the Internet and consequently was more productive, and I feel better about myself as a result. I didn't stop to think; I just wrote whatever came to my mind and kept the pen moving. Here are some of the things that showed up for me today.

- I'm thankful for everybody who recommended a book to me.
- I'm thankful to anyone who introduced me to someone from which a friendship has flourished or an acquaintance struck up.
- I'm thankful for sunglasses, silkworms, babies, air-conditioning, freshly squeezed orange juice, the library, books, the eye doctor, eyes, vision, the dentist, watermelon, electricity, Novocain, insect repellent, antibiotics, cutlery, *Tehillim*, music (Beethoven, Strauss, Brahms, Debussy, Tchaikovsky, Vivaldi, Rimsky-Korsakov, Ravel, folk music, Naomi Shemer), Shakespeare, Molière, Victor Hugo, Maupassant, Miss Rosenthal (my French teacher), Mrs. Shapiro (my Latin teacher), Dr. Rosmarin (my biology teacher), Rabbi Ellinson (my Hebrew teacher), Mrs. Davis,

my elementary school teacher who gave me a love for poetry and encouraged me to write when I was only ten years old, and Mrs. Pankhurst, my gym teacher, who had high standards and taught me to give it my all.

ATTITUDE IS EVERYTHING

I recently came across a story about the Baal Shem Tov.

It happened one day that he was walking with his students and encountered the town water carrier. He was bent over with a wooden pole on his back, a container filled with water on each side of the pole.

"How are you? How is business?" the Baal Shem Tov asked him.

"Terrible!" answered the water carrier. "It's such a hard, thankless job that I have. The water I carry is very heavy. It's backbreaking work that kills my back and shoulders. The work is menial and the pay is low. The townspeople look down at me, and if I come a few minutes late, they humiliate me."

The next day, the Baal Shem Tov went walking again with his students and again they met the water carrier.

"How are you? How's business?" the Baal Shem Tov asked him.

"I'm very happy," the water carrier answered.

"But yesterday you said things were terrible." The Baal Shem Tov was puzzled.

"I have a job. True, it doesn't pay much, but it necessitates me walking outdoors in the fresh air. That's healthy. I can put food on the table. I have what I need for myself and my family. I don't have to ask anyone for anything and I don't owe anyone anything. Life is good."

Happiness is not about what you have. It's about how you perceive what you have. And that is a choice all of us have.

GRATITUDE POEM I PENNED THE NIGHT AFTER YOM KIPPUR AT 4:30 A.M., OCTOBER 2003

The slate is clean

A new beginning

I can start afresh

The gift of a new day

I have no baggage from before

I have only today

I can make it be

The perfect day

I can live it

As if it were

The only day

Given to me to live

I can imbue it

With life and gratitude

Hour by hour

Minute by minute

A smile

A comforting word

Spoken to the right person

At the right moment

I smell a deep pink rose

And its aromatic fragrance heavenly

Fills me with awe and wonder

At the great Creator

Who made all this beauty

Just for me to enjoy

Its smooth silky petals

Soft as a baby's skin

Gently caress my cheeks

As I humbly bend my head

And recite the berachah

And praise the Almighty

With deep as the Grand Canyon

Gratitude

I walk away happy enriched

Keeping the exquisite

Scent of the rose

With me and within me

The rest of the day

I hear the chirp chirp chirp

Of the emerald green parrots

Who, dispossessed by Con Edison,[7]

Are busily rebuilding

Their nest anew

I watch them

Gathering twigs, leaves, and bits of string
and fluffy white cotton

Tidbits their razor-sharp eyes spot

On the sidewalk, in streets, gutters, and gardens

The other day I found two of them

Perched on my air-conditioner outside my bedroom window

With their eagle-like beaks

And their long emerald tails

They looked exotic

I saunter to the bus stop

Taking my time

It's a perfect day

The air is fresh

---

7   Con Edison destroyed the birds' nests on more than one occasion, because they felt the nests, which were huge, able to house twenty or more birds, were interfering with the electrical wires. Each time the birds rebuilt their nests but ultimately gave up.

It's not too hot

It's not too cold

The sun is shining

Benignly

As if God Himself

Is smiling

Confident that I will make this day

A day whose moments count

Moment by moment

My heart bursting with gratitude

I lower my head, bend my knees, bow to the Creator

And humbly declare

Hodu LaHashem ki Tov

Ki l'olam chasdo

Give thanks to God for He is good

For His loving-kindness endures forever

Epilogue

*Gratitude can work miracles in our lives,
transforming negative, self-defeating
thoughts into recognition of the gifts
life has to offer.*

Melody Beattie

I HAVE FOUND that the more I practice gratitude, the more joyful and generally happier I become. That is not to say I never have a low mood, a day or patches when things just don't seem to be going right, or periods of existential loneliness—but though extremely painful, these don't usually last quite as long as they used to.

An interesting and most gratifying outcome of my gratitude practice is that I am not so stuck in perceiving things in only one way as I was wont to do. I find my cognition is more fluid, so that if I encounter a situation that I could well do without, instead of fretting, worrying, and wallowing in self-pity, an idea will suddenly pop into my head quite effortlessly. I see another, more positive aspect of that situation, which means I'm not stuck with one perspective. I see that things are not necessarily the way they appear to be; there are different facets.

Because I am becoming less rigid in my thinking, I am more creative, and if I get hurt (and who doesn't at some time in their life?), I find I am able to forgive more readily, let it go, and move on, because I recognize there are many different ways to see a particular situation. Perhaps the person offending my sensibilities didn't mean to upset or hurt me, per-haps they are going through a difficult patch in their life which creates impatience and lack of empathy in them, perhaps they said something in jest and I took it too seriously.

Over these many years that I have consciously been striving to live in gratitude, I am becoming less judgmental, more open-minded and more accepting of situations and people. I notice I am giving people space to be who they are more of the time. Gratitude has impacted me in multiple wonderful ways. I am becoming less critical of people and even of myself, more understanding, more loving, more generous, more joyful, more optimistic, and more energized.

It is my fervent wish that this book will help you, my readers, develop your own practice of gratitude, so that you, too, will reap its far-reaching benefits: enhanced interpersonal relationships, improved health, less stress, more resilience, and more joy and optimism, and find inner peace, contentment, and a deeper connection to God.

The time to start is now. Don't postpone for even one moment. Start to practice gratitude and enjoy life to the fullest.

Appendix I

Here are two calendars to help you live in gratitude consciousness on a daily basis.

Day 1 What are you grateful for today?	Day 2 What is something someone said to you today that you are grateful for?	Day 3 What article of clothing are you grateful for?	Day 4 What thing in your bedroom are you grateful for?	Day 5 What sound are you grateful for?	Day 6 Which of your possessions are you grateful for?	Day 7 What memory are you grateful for?
Day 8 Which of your relatives are you grateful for today?	Day 9 What color are you grateful for today?	Day 10 What food are you grateful for today?	Day 11 What music are you grateful for today?	Day 12 What book have you read that you are grateful for?	Day 13 What gift are you grateful for?	Day 14 What is something that someone said to you that you are grateful for?
Day 15 What did you see in nature today that you are grateful for?	Day 16 What did you do to help someone today that made them happy?	Day 17 What hobby are you grateful for?	Day 18 What movie did you see that you are grateful for?	Day 19 What game are you grateful for?	Day 20 Who were you kind to today? What did you do that was kind?	Day 21 What made you happy today that you are grateful for?
Day 22 What made you happy last week that you are grateful for?	Day 23 What was the nicest thing your mother said to you that you are grateful for?	Day 24 What was the nicest thing your father said to you that you are grateful for?	Day 25 What was the nicest thing your teacher did that you are grateful for?	Day 26 What was the nicest thing you said to your mother that you are grateful for?	Day 27 What was the nicest thing you said to your father that you are grateful for?	Day 28 What is the nicest thing you said to your friend that you are grateful for?
Day 29 What was the best trip your family took that you are grateful for?	Day 30 What was your nicest birthday party that you are grateful for?	Day 31 Why is gratitude important?				

Day 1 Write a gratitude letter to your mother	*Day 2* Write a gratitude letter to your father	*Day 3* Write a Thank You letter to your brother	*Day 4* Write a Thank You letter to your sister	*Day 5* Write a Thank You letter to a friend	*Day 6* Write a Thank You letter to your teacher	*Day 7* Write a Thank You letter to your grandparents
Day 8 Meditate for five minutes on loving-kindnesses you have received	*Day 9* Do a random act of kindness for a total stranger	*Day 10* Write a Thank You letter to your mailman	*Day 11* Write a Thank You letter to our president	*Day 12* Visit a homebound senior citizen	*Day 13* Write a Thank You letter to a neighbor	*Day 14* Treat yourself today as you would treat a cherished friend
Day 15 Draw a picture of something you appreciate in nature	*Day 16* Make a list of five things you are grateful for	*Day 17* Make a list of four books you have read, that you are grateful for	*Day 18* Write a letter to an author of a book that you enjoyed reading	*Day 19* Be extra patient and forgiving today	*Day 20* Look in the mirror, smile and say, "I am enough, I have enough"	*Day 21* Write a letter of appreciation to your child
Day 22 Call a friend and share ten things you are grateful for	*Day 23* Do something nice for a sibling	*Day 24* Bake a cake for your child's teacher	*Day 25* Write a letter to your child's principal praising her teacher	*Day 26* Compose a gratitude poem	*Day 27* Sing and dance for a few minutes today	*Day 28* Draw or paint a gratitude picture
Day 29 Volunteer at a soup kitchen for the homeless	*Day 30* Visit patients at a hospital	*Day 31* Replace worry with faith and trust today				

Appendix II
Prayers of Gratitude

THANK YOU HASHEM, King of Kings and Master of the World!

Thank You for the infinite times that You helped me, supported me, rescued me, encouraged me, cured me, guarded over me, and made me happy.

Thank You for always being with me.

Thank You for giving me the strength to observe Your commandments, to do good deeds and pray. Thank You for all the times You helped me and I didn't know how to say "Thank You."

Thank You for all the loving kindnesses You do for me each and every moment.

Thank You for every breath I breathe.

Thank You Hashem for all the things that I do have, and thank You Hashem even for the things I don't have.

Thank You for my periodic difficulties, my occasional setbacks, and for the times when I don't feel happy, because everything is for my ultimate benefit, even if I don't see that it's always for my best...

Deep in my heart, I know that everything that comes from You is the very best for me and designed especially for me in precision and exacting Divine Providence, of which only the King of Kings is capable.

Thank You for the periodic times that are difficult for me, for only that way they enable me to fully appreciate the good times, for only after being in darkness one can appreciate the light.

Thank You for the wonderful life You have given me.

Thank You for every little thing that I have, for everything comes from You and from no one else.

Thank You for always listening to my prayers.

Creator of the World, I apologize from the bottom of my heart for all the times that I didn't appreciate what You gave me, and instead of thanking You, I only complained.

I am dust and ashes, and You are the entire universe. Please, don't ever cast me away.

About the Author

SARAH BERKOVITS, acclaimed, innovative, and creative educator and public speaker, has taught at some of the most prestigious schools in England, Israel, and America, including Hasmonean Prep, Evelina de Rothschild, Ramaz Upper School, and the Yeshiva of Flatbush. She was also a psychology professor at Touro College.

For twenty-eight years, Sarah served as a nationally certified clinical counselor for the NYC Department of Education, ultimately becoming a consultant and staff development trainer. She is the author of *Guided Imagery with Children: Successful Techniques to Improve School Performance and Self-Esteem* (Whole Person Associates). Currently, she divides her time between writing, consulting, and public speaking. She also has a private psychotherapy practice.

Ms. Berkovits would be happy to hear from her readers. She can be reached at ssb316@msn.com.

MOSAICA PRESS

BOOK PUBLISHERS

Elegant, Meaningful & Bold

info@MosaicaPress.com
www.MosaicaPress.com

The Mosaica Press team of
acclaimed editors and designers
is attracting some of the most
compelling thinkers and teachers
in the Jewish community today.
Our books are available around
the world.

HARAV YAACOV HABER
RABBI DORON KORNBLUTH